My Most Memorable Races

MY MOST MEMORABLE RACES

Peter Bromley

Stanley Paul
London Melbourne Auckland Johannesburg

Stanley Paul & Co. Ltd

An imprint of Century Hutchinson Ltd

62–65 Chandos Place, London WC2N 4NW

Century Hutchinson Australia (Pty) Ltd
PO Box 496, 16–22 Church Street, Hawthorn, Melbourne, Victoria 3122

Century Hutchinson New Zealand Limited
PO Box 40–086, Glenfield, Auckland 10

Century Hutchinson South Africa (Pty) Ltd
PO Box 337, Bergvlei 2012, South Africa

First published 1988

Set in Linotron Sabon by Input Typesetting, London
Printed in Great Britain by
Anchor Brendon, Tiptree, Essex

British Library Cataloguing in Publication Data

Bromley, Peter
My most memorable races.
1. Racehorses. Racing. Races, 1960–1987
I. Title
798.4'009'04

ISBN 0 09 163860 7

Contents

Acknowledgements vii
Introduction xi
1960 Two Thousand Guineas – *Martial* 1
1962 Northumberland Plate – *Bordone* 6
1964 Gold Cup – *Arkle and Mill House* 9
1965 Grand National – *Jay Trump and Freddie* 15
1965 Derby – *Sea Bird* 20
1970 Prix de l'Arc de Triomphe – *Sassafras and Nijinsky* 24
1971 Two Thousand Guineas – *Brigadier Gerard* 34
1971 Prix de l'Arc de Triomphe – *Mill Reef* 40
1973 Grand National – *Red Rum and Crisp* 44
1973 Finch Decanter Stakes – *Wrens Hill* 50
1974 One Thousand Guineas – *Highclere* 52
1975 King George VI and Queen Elizabeth Diamond Stakes – *Grundy and Bustino* 56
1975 St Leger – *Bruni* 62
1977 *News of the World* Grand National – *Red Rum* 65
Speed and Stamina at Royal Ascot 73
1979 and 1981 Waterford Crystal Champion Hurdle – *Monksfield and Sea Pigeon* 79
1980 Spillers Stewards Cup – *Repetitious* 88
1981 Sun Grand National – *Aldaniti* 91
1981 Derby – *Shergar* 99
1984 Whitbread Gold Cup – *Special Cargo* 101
Lester Piggott 107

1985 General Accident One Thousand Guineas – *Oh So Sharp* 114
1986 Tote Cheltenham Gold Cup – *Dawn Run* 118
1986 THF Prix de l'Arc de Triomphe – *Dancing Brave* 124
Cauthen's Classics 129
1987 Dresden Diamond Stakes – *Ten No Trumps* 137
The Finish 141
Bibliography 143

Acknowledgements

Many people have helped me in the preparation of this book and I am grateful to those who have looked back and searched their memories in order to provide a new insight into the races that I have chosen.

I am deeply indebted to David McCall for giving his time to recount the inside story of Nijinsky's defeat in the Prix de l'Arc de Triomphe, a shock which undermined the already fragile state of owner Charles Engelhard's health.

Grant Pritchard-Gordon, racing manager to Prince Khalid Abdullah kindly gave me much background information to Dancing Brave's fabulous victory in the Arc.

I am grateful to Ian Balding, who told me new and hitherto unknown facts concerning Mill Reef's defeat in the Two Thousand Guineas and his preparation for his famous success in the Arc.

Joe Mercer, with immense pride, recalled the glorious day at Chantilly when, in the presence of her owner and breeder, Her Majesty The Queen, Highclere rose to the occasion and gave a British Monarch a first success in a French Classic. That must have been Joe's greatest moment in a long and distinguished career which I have so much admired. Joe also helped over the tale of the Two Thousand Guineas which he won on Brigadier Gerard, one of sixteen wins in seventeen races on that great horse.

Those sterling supporters of National Hunt racing, Reg and Betty Tweedie, reminded me of the 'heady' days of Freddie and the Grand National trophy that they so nearly took back to Kelso.

Ron Hutchinson recalled his days at Paddy Prendergast's stable, and the occasion that I am sure he will never forget when Martial gave him his first English Classic on his first ride in England.

Richard Pitman, like Dick Francis, came within a few yards of seeing a dream come true at Aintree only to have it transferred cruelly into a nightmare. I am sure that the moment is still painful to endure, so I wish to record my thanks for his help over Crisp's magnificent run in the National and his sensational defeat by the 'greatest horse of Aintree', Red Rum. Tommy Stack, now a stud manager in Ireland, provided me with details of Red Rum's record third National win. While most of us were making our way home, Southport was *en fête*, and Tommy must have been bemused at the way that this historic victory was celebrated.

In deciding which of the many Champion Hurdles that I have described, I was led straight to the 1979 race through Jonathan Powell's vivid description on the opening page of his delightful book, *Monksfield*. Jonathan was also responsible for the moving story of Bob Champion's fight against cancer in *Champion's Story*, and I am extremely grateful for permission to quote passages from both his books. Bill Curling's book *Sea Pigeon* also yielded much valuable information on the 1981 Waterford Crystal Champion Hurdle.

Ian de Wesselow has most generously given permission to reproduce from *Raceform* the results of the 30 races which I have described. *Raceform* is the official Jockey Club record of racing results and, with the *Raceform Note-book*, is an indispensible aid for the professional racing world.

Another racing publication on my bookshelf is *Timeform's Racehorses Annuals*. This is indeed a treasury of racing knowledge: it represents a complete history of the post-war period, and I am constantly delving into one or other of the volumes and often become distracted by one of the illuminating essays on a particular topic. The comments on Nijinsky, Sea Bird and Slip Anchor from the 1965, 1970 and 1985 editions are very appropriate, and I am grateful to Reg Griffin, managing director of *Timeform*, for permission to quote from them. Perhaps the most astonishing part of *Timeform's Racehorses Annuals* is the standard of excellence which has been maintained throughout its long and distinguished history. What, I wonder, did racing correspondents do before the era of *Timeform?*

Bill Smith was kind enough to give me the background story to the 1984 Whitbread Gold Cup, in which he rode Diamond Edge instead of the winner from the same stable, Special Cargo. His disappointment at failing to create a record three wins in the race on his final ride must surely be tempered by the sight of Her Majesty The Queen Mother receiving the trophy she was herself to have presented.

Jimmy Lindley gave me considerable encouragement. He helped over the chapter on Steve Cauthen's Classics and made many observations which I have incorporated in the book.

My thanks to photographers George Selwyn, David Hastings, Sport & General Press Agency and Keystone Collection for permission to reproduce their photographs.

I am extremely grateful to Annette Maiden, who read the manuscript in the early stages and made some most helpful suggestions. My colleague John Haslam from Radio Outside Broadcasts and now Assistant Press Secretary to The Queen, has tried to make my English more readable. It has all been put together by Dominique Shead, and to her and everyone else who has contributed towards these memorable races, I wish to record my most sincere thanks.

Introduction

It was quite a shock to the system to be reminded before the 1985 Ever Ready Derby won by Slip Anchor that it was going to be the twenty-fifth Derby that I had commentated on for BBC Radio. Psidium, the 66 to 1 winner in 1961, had been the first and the time in between yielded a host of vivid memories.

Roddy Bloomfield, the publisher of my first book *The Price of Success*, has frequently managed to squeeze into my commentary box high in the Epsom grandstand and has shared many of those moments from the windy perch of Box No 1 in the Grand Tier, an exposed pitch much beloved of pigeons. Roddy remarked that, as a quarter of a century of racing history had gone past my nose, it might be appropriate to write about my most memorable races.

That was quite a challenge, for in addition to the 124 Classic races that I have had the privilege of describing, there have also been 25 Gold Cups, the same number of Champion Hurdles and Grand Nationals, not to mention the King George VI and Queen Elizabeth Stakes, assorted 'Arcs' and any number of group races and big betting handicaps.

In the end there turned out to be a list of some 500 races to choose from; what were to be the criteria? Some races I can remember quite vividly for purely personal reasons which may be of not the slightest interest to the reader, while others qualify for inclusion because of the closeness of the finish or the quality of the horses taking part. Arkle, Sea Bird, Nijinsky, Brigadier Gerard, Mill Reef and Dancing Brave must feature in any account of racing over the last eventful twenty-five years.

Perhaps the most memorable to me of all races was on the occasion of my first radio commentary for BBC Radio, down the course for the Newmarket Stakes on 13 May 1959. I had worked for five years on the panel of racecourse commentators employed by Broadcast Amplifiers, a Brighton-based firm which supplied the public address systems for most racecourses. So I had already worked from the ditch position at Newmarket from a hut, but now being perched precariously on the roof of the BBC van in a high wind was something new. I felt insecure, it was difficult to keep my binoculars steady and, worst of all, within a few seconds of starting my minor part in the broadcast, the wind whipped my notes from under the clip on my mill-board; away they swept across the open heath like confetti. I felt naked and vulnerable, and was subsequently responsible for the longest 'pause' ever on steam radio.

Although there were only five runners, my mind went numb and I could not remember a single thing to say about them. Eventually, after what seemed a lifetime, I picked up the threads and described the favourite, Masham, lining up for the start with the eventual winner, Agricola, ridden by 'Manny' Mercer.

The Head of Outside Broadcasts, Charles Max Muller, wrote to me later saying that he thought that my first broadcast had gone quite well *but* that there had been a long, and for radio an unacceptable pause when Raymond Glendenning had handed over to me. I honestly believed that I had 'blown it', but that initial catastrophe taught me a most valuable lesson. I had to be prepared to talk and to go on talking no matter what conditions were like and in spite of any horrors that might occur. From that day onward I have always used cardboard for my racecard and notes and always carry a spare racecard in my left-hand pocket. I did once drop my mill-board with the racecard clipped to it over the edge of the parapet at York, just before the Ebor Handicap, but on that occasion the second racecard was in place and I was able to use it for reference.

In the summer of 1959 I was offered the post of BBC

Racing Correspondent, the first accredited sports correspondent. The post was shared by radio and television, though to begin with I spent more time at Shepherds Bush with programmes such as *Sportsview* and *Grandstand*. My regular stint was to be the 'third man' in the television racing team, acting as back-up and understudy for race commentator Peter O'Sullevan and paddock commentator Clive Graham, the most experienced and professional team on television. I was also responsible for giving the pre-race betting and the starting prices from a specially adapted Land Rover which was parked alongside the television scanner. After the race I would leap out and interview the winning jockey, owner or trainer. There was never a dull moment, and there were some distinctly anxious ones: I remember the sight of Ronnie Pantlin, the floor manager, standing by the side of the camera with his hand raised, while I stood alone in the winners' enclosure without a subject to interview.

On one occasion, with nothing on my mind other than the anticipation of enjoying the Goodwood August meeting, I arrived at the racecourse at about eleven o'clock to be greeted by the Assistant Head of Outside Broadcasts, Harry Middleton, and the BBC Radio racing producer Henry Riddell. They appeared anxious. Raymond Glendenning had been taken ill and I was to do the Stewards Cup for radio. It had all been arranged with Peter Dimmock, and I could do this in addition to my normal television routine.

I had never before worked at Goodwood, which was the first course to have running commentaries over the public address system. This technique had been developed by Bob Haynes, an ex-Guardsman and a quite brilliant and accurate race-reader, whose modulated clear voice set the standard and pattern for all other commentators, with a delivery that was unhurried and easy for racegoers to follow. Bob had always done Goodwood commentaries, and so I embarked on the Stewards Cup, one of the big betting handicaps of the year, without ever having worked there.

The BBC Radio commentary point was at the extreme

left-hand end of the top level of the Private Stand, but quite close to the Judges' Box and therefore to the finishing line. Many of the members who viewed the races from this part of the stand knew each other and were nearly all members of the 'Twelve Club'. They all knew Raymond Glendenning, and they did not seem too sure about the inexperienced young man who had taken over.

I now discovered, for the first time, that the start of the Stewards Cup is out of sight from even the top of the Grandstand, lying in 'dead' ground beyond the ridge at the five-furlong point. This compounded the difficulty, for the field cover almost a furlong before they come into view, spread out across the course like charging cavalry. It is quite the most unnerving seventy-two seconds of the commentator's year.

From the field of twenty runners, two horses drew away from the rest in the last two furlongs. They were the favourite Deer Leap, ridden by Greville Starkey, and Monet, ridden by Jimmy Lindley. They flashed past the post locked together and I called Monet the winner in a photo finish. The Judge, John Hancock, called for a photograph and Roger Mortimer, who was the regular summariser, helped me to fill in the time while the photo was being developed. After a five-minute wait my confidence in my ability to judge the result from a position I had never before used began to ebb away, and after another three minutes with no announcement I was prepared to settle for a dead heat. To my immense relief, and I dare say that of everyone in the Outside Broadcast Department, Monet was given as the winner and Deer Leap was again second. (He had been runner-up to Sir Winston Churchill's Tudor Monarch the previous year and in 1961 he was second for the third year running – he had been beaten by a short head, a neck and a short head in three Stewards Cups.) He was later sold for 9000 guineas as a stallion for Poland. I had a very soft spot for Deer Leap afterwards. His defeat by a few inches had helped me on to a new career in radio.

1960
Two Thousand Guineas

Martial

The 1960 Two Thousand Guineas is also indelibly etched in my memory, even though I described only part of the race from the roof of the BBC van, six furlongs from the finish, as the 'down the course' commentator. Martial's exceptionally dramatic win for Ireland in a photo finish had the effect of assisting me to become the radio Grandstand commentator rather more quickly than I might otherwise have expected.

In the spring of 1960 I worked rather more for BBC Television than I did for radio, under the editor of *Grandstand*, Paul Fox, and the deputy editor Ronnie Noble. They were both very keen on racing and on showing preview film in *Sportsview* of horses being prepared for the big races that would eventually feature in *Grandstand*. In that spring it seemed that the two principal Irish trainers, Vincent O'Brien and Paddy Prendergast, might sweep all before them in the coming season. It was decided to send Ronnie Noble and me together with a camera crew to film both stables.

Both trainers were extremely enthusiastic and co-operated whole-heartedly. Coverage of training horses on television was something quite new, and at the Curragh Paddy Prendergast allowed the camera car to track alongside his Guineas candidates, Martial and Paddy's Sister. The latter had won the Queen Mary and then beaten the colts in both the Gimcrack Stakes and the Champagne Stakes. She was the top-rated filly in the Free Handicap and winter favourite for the One Thousand Guineas.

Martial, who had won the Coventry Stakes and had returned home with sore shins, did not race again as a two-year-old. He had grown into a most powerful three-year-old, muscular, thick-set and heavy topped, with a tremendous shoulder. As I watched him work, ridden by the new Australian jockey Ron Hutchinson, from a car alongside, I was struck by the awesome power he exuded as he was restrained so skilfully. I certainly did not envy Ron Hutchinson sitting astride this great machine trying to bore a hole in the horizon.

We interviewed both Paddy Prendergast and Ron Hutchinson, who was fresh from Melbourne where he was the leading rider. 'Hutch', as he later became known, was then thirty-three years old and he was following in the tracks of other successful Australian jockeys who had come to ride in Europe, such as Scobie Breasley, Bill Williamson and George Moore. Seeing Hutch riding work suggested that he would be just as successful as the others, for he sat very close to his horse and looked very neat and accomplished. During our visit he expressed one deep concern – that he was going to ride fancied horses at Newmarket but had never even seen the course. At that stage I was contracted to do the Guineas from 'down the course', so I offered to walk the Rowley Mile with Ron on the day before the Two Thousand Guineas.

While we were preparing the film, we learnt that Paddy's Sister was not going to run and so there was some last-minute editing. I had already backed Martial at 33 to 1, and coupled him with Paddy's Sister. Meanwhile, the Two Thousand Guineas was building up into a very fine race. Favourite was the Middle Park winner Venture VI owned by Prince Aly Khan and trained by Alec Head at Chantilly.

The news from Ireland concerning Martial was not particularly encouraging. A dry spring with cold winds had made the going hard at the Curragh, and I learnt that Paddy Prendergast was having difficulty getting this huge horse fit, and had been sending him to the sands in Dublin Bay for fast gallops. Neither did his form in the Thirsk Classic Trial strike terror into the hearts of the bookmakers, for he was beaten three lengths by Newbus.

As the Two Thousand Guineas drew closer there was no change in the weather in Ireland, and Paddy Prendergast sent Martial over to Newmarket under the care of Bernard van Cutsem a week early in the hope that the Newmarket ground would be better. In fact it was now firm at Newmarket, and Martial drifted in the betting.

I do not think that Ron Hutchinson was very confident when I took him down the course to walk the Rowley mile. Drawn one in a field of seventeen, we walked the whole way down the standside rails. In those days almost the entire course was used, with a temporary running rail a few yards in from the stands rails. I pointed out to Ron the classic way of using the downhill run from the Bushes to gain impetus for the rising ground in the last furlong and a half, and impressed upon him the need to keep on riding up to the post and not to try to guess whether or not he was in front of the horses racing so wide from him over on the far side of the course. Hutchinson was astonished at the width of the course and did not seem able to believe that there would be two groups of horses so widely separated.

The Alec Head-trained Venture VI went off the 6 to 4 favourite, with St Paddy, running for the first time, at 5 to 1; Martial drifted out to 18 to 1. This was Ron Hutchinson's first ride at Newmarket and he immediately took Martial to the front of the small group that remained on the stands side. As the field passed me, perched dangerously on the roof of the van, Geoff Lewis led overall on Filipepi on the far side.

In what seemed like a brief instant my part was over and I handed to Raymond Glendenning in the Grandstand, but I continued to watch the horses, widely separated by the width of the Rowley Mile. At the Bushes the runners were momentarily lost from sight but I heard Raymond call Venture coming away on the far side to win from Auroy, Tulyartos, High Hat and St Paddy. I could see that Martial had won the race on the stands side, but he was not called in the first four. Driving back in the car to the Grandstand I was not best pleased. My Irish reconnaissance had not so far paid any dividends, and with Paddy's Sister a non-runner in the One Thousand Guineas there would be some nasty bills to come.

When I entered the unsaddling enclosure, to my astonishment I saw Paddy Prendergast holding court to a crowd of journalists. Peter O'Sullevan came over and said 'Why didn't you keep your big mouth shut?' I was still unaware of what had happened, and my first question to Peter was, 'Has there been an objection?' He replied, 'Martial won the race and Ron Hutchinson said that without your help he would not have won. I have backed Venture VI and he finished on the far side and was beaten a head.' I explained to Peter that I had been listening to Raymond Glendenning, who had told the world that Venture VI had won, while Martial was never mentioned.

Hutch came out and thanked me for the local knowledge that he had gained and put to such good use. Later I learnt that George Moore had been looking across at Martial throughout the last hundred yards, but Hutch had put his head down and did not stop riding until he reached the end of the boards by the side of the paddock, at least fifty yards past the post. Martial's astonishing late run up the hill had caught out George Moore and, sadly, Raymond Glendenning who had obviously been concentrating on the far-side group and had missed Martial racing on the stands side.

In those days the BBC Radio commentary position was at the first-floor roof level, far too low down and at least fifty yards from the winning post. For years Raymond had struggled with huge fields in races such as the Cambridgeshire from a position that made it virtually impossible to give an accurate judgement. (The Jockey Club was at that time obsessed by the possibility of a commentator disagreeing with the Judge's verdict, and there were orders that no one apart from the Judge was to be allowed to be positioned on the winning line.) One of the first things that I did when I took over from him was to survey all our commentary boxes, and to have them moved to more satisfactory positions. When I gave the commentary on the Two Thousand Guineas the following year from the Grandstand, it was from a new custom-built commentary box on the roof and as close to the line as I was permitted. I have been there ever since.

Ron Hutchinson had therefore won a Classic on his first ride in Britain, and he continued from that successful start to set up a quite remarkable record by scoring at Chester, Royal Ascot, Goodwood, York and Doncaster on his very first visits to those courses. After two seasons with Paddy Prendergast he came to Britain and rode for the Duke and Duchess of Norfolk.

NEWMARKET, Wed., Apr. 27th 1960 (Firm)
2000 GUINEAS STAKES £16,854 1m 3.10

MARTIAL 9–0	RHutchinson	–1
Venture VII 9–0	GMoore	hd.2
Auroy 9–0	TGosling	4.3
Tulyartos 9–0	WWilliamson	½.4
High Hat 9–0	WCarr	½.5
St Paddy 9–0	LPiggott	¾.6

S.P.: 6/4 Venture VII, 5/1 St Paddy, 11/2 Filipepi, 100/9 Newbus, 100/8 Red Gauntlet, 100/7 Tudorich, 18/1 MARTIAL, 20/1 Tulyartos. (Mr R. N. Webster) P. Prendergast, Ireland. 17 Rn 1m 38.33

1962
Northumberland Plate

Bordone

In my early days as the BBC Radio racing commentator, the North Region was extremely keen to broadcast races from the northern racecourses. Aintree, Chester and Doncaster were all covered and one of the most popular events was the Northumberland Plate, known as the Pitmans Derby. This two-mile handicap was considered locally as important as the Melbourne Cup is in Australia. My second visit to Newcastle to broadcast the race commentary was an unmitigated disaster.

I arrived early at the course to check on the facilities and the commentary point. The BBC had hired a private box for the day from the owner but I was worried that the long-range binoculars which I had inherited from Raymond Glendenning were rather unsteadily mounted on a wooden tripod which could be erected only on level ground at the back of the box. All went well until the runners were on their way to the start, when into the box swept a dozen noisy friends of the owner who always watched from this box. Unfortunately, no one had told them that it was not available on this day.

The unwelcome guests crowded to the front of the box regardless of the fact that it must have been patently obvious that a live broadcast was being conducted. The producer in charge seemed powerless to remove the racegoers, and so I was forced to abandon the pitch with the big ex-German naval glasses and elbow my way to the front of the box, picking up my own 7 by 50 binoculars.

By now the race was on, and when I levelled my glasses on the leaders, to my horror I could see two distinct sets of runners. The prism in one eyepiece had become dislodged and I was literally seeing double. After seconds of blind panic I discovered which lens was floating, closed that eye and proceeded with my commentary using one eye.

This was a drama I had not up until now encountered, and I still had to fight for room to see at the front of the box. It was a desperate finish and I described Bordone and Optimistic flashing past the post locked together in a photograph, with the other racegoers shouting and screaming and jostling all around me. To rub salt into the wound, one of the more strident women in the box banged me on the shoulder and asked me what had won. I told her, and probably half a million listeners as well, that I did not know and we would have to wait for the Judge to announce the result.

The Royal horse Optimistic was beaten by a short head by Bordone and I returned listeners to the studio with intense relief. The broadcast had been a shambles and I have never had any desire to listen to it again. What is quite extraordinary is that no one complained by writing to or telephoning the BBC about either the standard of the commentary or the incessant noise during the race.

Indeed, only one person raised the matter. Paddy Prendergast had a runner, Multy, ridden by Peader Mathews, which was unplaced. The next time I saw Paddy he asked me, 'What was up with you at Newcastle? You were terrible.' When I recounted the story I thought that he would do himself an injury laughing. The late Paddy Prendergast had a delicious sense of humour, but it was some time before I was able to bring myself to laugh at the events at the Plate in 1962.

NEWCASTLE, Sat., Jun. 30th (Good)
NORTHUMBERLAND PLATE (H'Cap) £5,045 2m 3.40

BORDONE 4–8–5	GLittlewood	–1
Optimistic 5–8–5	DWMorriss	s.hd.2
Sostenuto 4–8–11	Don Morris	1.3
Avon's Pride 5–9–6	JLindley	5.4

Rainstorm 5–7–7	BRaymond	4.5
Utrillo 5–8–6	JMullane	s.hd.6

S.P.: 4/1 Avon's Pride, 9/2 Optimistic, 8/1 Highland Fusilier, 9/1 Parnear, 10/1 Sunny Way, Royal Glen, 100/9 Rainstorm, 100/8 Utrillo, Hard Master, 100/7 BORDONE, 100/6 Touch Wood, 25/1 Sostenuto. (Mr A. B. Grant) G. Fenningworth, Richmond, Yorks. 13 Rn 3m 32.10

1964
Gold Cup

Arkle and Mill House

In the sixties one horse so dominated the National Hunt scene that he became a legend. Even now it is hard to pass his statue at Cheltenham without spending a few moments in silent homage to this great chaser. For three years he was the master of the game, revered and admired; he brought National Hunt racing to many people who would otherwise not have taken any notice. In Anne, Duchess of Westminster he had the perfect owner, and gave just reward for the patience and patronage that she had lavished on her favourite sport of steeplechasing.

I remember both Arkle's first and last races in England with a vividness that I find truly remarkable. I watched the Honeybourne Chase at Cheltenham on 17 November 1962 from a point down the course, at the second-last fence. On the first circuit Pat Taaffe had his arms pulled out by this powerful galloper, and to my astonishment Arkle was still pulling just as hard the second time round and Pat was still restraining him shouting, 'Whoa boy'. Arkle pulled himself clear of a useful field to win unchallenged by twenty lengths. I returned to the weighing room and I remember talking to Francis Byrne, that most knowledgeable writer for *The Times*, and telling him what I had seen down the course. He said that Tom Dreaper had told him that this was the best horse he had trained since Prince Regent.

Arkle's last race was, I think, the saddest day I have known. It was the 1966 King George VI Chase at Kempton Park. The Boxing Day card had had to be abandoned due to frost, but the King George VI Chase was carried over to Tuesday 27 December. Because of the change BBC

Radio was not covering the race, so I went as an observer. I took my neighbour Dr James Arkle and we watched the race together from the members' seated accommodation. There was still fog lingering on the course and it was impossible to see the colours over on the far side, but six fences from home, at fence 14, Arkle seemed hardly to rise at the fence and he lost the lead. He battled back and regained the lead, but went under to the 10 to 1 chance Dormant, beaten by only a length. He pulled up very lame and it was clear as he returned to the unsaddling enclosure that he had run the last mile on only three sound legs.

It was later discovered after X-rays that he had cracked a pedal bone when striking the take-off board of the fourteenth fence. His trainer Tom Dreaper had returned to Ireland and he was represented by his wife, Betty. At this awful moment when it became apparent that the great, invincible Arkle was crippled, two trainers came to assist Mrs Dreaper, Frank Cundell (a veterinary surgeon) and Ryan Price. Together they helped the racecourse vet to bandage the damaged foot and leg and to get Arkle on to a low trailer to be taken to the racecourse stables. It did not look good, and I took Pat Taaffe to London Airport to catch his flight back to Dublin. He was in tears as it became clear, on that foggy night, that his long and so successful partnership with Arkle had ended.

In the intervening three years – 1964, 1965 and 1966 – of Arkle's reign he gave me an embarrassing number of memorable races to chronicle. All three of his Cheltenham Gold Cup wins were remarkable and resulted in scenes of unprecedented enthusiasm from the Irish visitors. Also outstanding were his extraordinary weight-carrying achievements in handicaps. He won the 1965 Whitbread Gold Cup at Sandown under 12.7 and the Gallagher Gold Cup under 12.7 by twenty lengths, knocking 17 seconds off the course record. Arkle was now presenting the handicappers with a tremendous problem: they really needed a weight scale of four stone. The 1964 and 1965 Hennessy Gold Cups fell to him under 12.7 but in 1966 he failed by only half a length to give 35 lb to Stalbridge Colonist, who subsequently finished second and third in the Gold Cup.

This defeat at Newbury was probably Arkle's finest race, only one month before his last tragic race and most courageous performance in the King George VI Chase. He won twenty-seven of his thirty-five races and earned more than £75,000. I was privileged to describe twelve of his fifteen races in England on BBC Radio. The Honeybourne Chase and Broadway Chase which Arkle won in the 1962/3 season were not broadcast, and neither was the King George VI Chase transferred from Boxing Day in 1966. It is hard to choose which race was the most memorable, but I have decided on the 1964 Cheltenham Gold Cup.

The Race

The build-up for the Gold Cup concerned the re-match of two chasers, the 1963 winner of the Blue Riband, Mill House, and Ireland's exciting new young chaser Arkle. Even though Arkle had gone through his Novice chase season unbeaten in all his five races over fences, in the Hennessy the handicapper had set him to receive 5 lb from Mill House, who started the 13 to 8 favourite, with Arkle at 5 to 2.

Mill House was everyone's idea of what a chaser should look like – big and powerful with a majestic stride, and a magnificent jumper. His partner was William Robinson, one of the best jockeys to come from Ireland. Robinson's style was unique: he sat very still and quiet, and he had the most perfect hands and the tactical brain of a flat-race jockey. Indeed, he had ridden with distinction on the flat, riding Paddy's Point into second place in the 1958 Derby which was won by Hard Ridden. Under National Hunt rules he rode the winners of the Champion Hurdle, the Gold Cup and the Grand National.

Hennessy day at Newbury had been cold and foggy – visibility for the race was down to the last fence. I had read practically the entire race from the television monitor (black and white in those days), with a mackintosh over my head to try to get the best possible picture. I had been able to see the catastrophic mistake that Arkle made at the third fence from home, the last open ditch. He slipped on landing, almost fell and though out of contention he struggled on to finish third, beaten three-quarters of a length and eight lengths by Mill House. Arkle had been lying second when he blundered, and after the race Pat Taaffe said that he would have won. Due to the atrocious visibility, many had been unaware of Arkle's mistake and so they perhaps gave Mill House rather more credit for his win than he had merited.

For the Gold Cup, therefore, there was a score to settle, and for the Irish punters some Newbury losses to recover. Arkle's defeat there had broken a run of eight consecutive wins.

There was a great air of expectancy on the final day of the National Hunt Festival, where the Irish presence helps to make Cheltenham a very special place for my favourite three days' racing of the year. It was Mill House versus Arkle, England versus Ireland, conveniently forgetting of course that Mill House and his jockey were also bred in Ireland. Still, Mill House was now trained in Lambourn, and had he not already won the Gold Cup the year before?

It was a glorious day for the race, cold but bright and sunny with perfect visibility, and walking around before the race it seemed that there were probably very few people left in Ireland: they were all here to cheer Arkle. But Mill House was the 13 to 8 on favourite – he had jumped Arkle almost down at Newbury and given him 5 lb and an eight-and-three-quarter-length beating. He was being spoken of as the new Golden Miller. His supporters had seen him win the King George at Kempton on Boxing Day, and they would not hear of defeat.

Although there was a field of four, only the big two mattered, and Kings Nephew was at 20 to 1 and Pas Seul at 50 to 1.

The tactics of the race were predictable: Mill House would try to capitalise on his superb jumping, while Arkle would try to wait on the big horse and 'do him for speed' between the last two fences.

I was staying at the same Cheltenham Hotel as Pat Taaffe and Willie Robinson. They were great friends, and both seemed extraordinarily confident. They were also extremely relaxed, and when I breakfasted with them I admit to being the most nervous of the three of us about the afternoon's race.

My breakfast nerves had not gone by post time and I felt unusually tense, even with such a small field. I am sure that the importance of this particular Gold Cup had got through to me. Remember, too, that at this stage Arkle had run only twice in Britain, winning the Broadway Chase the previous year and being beaten in the Hennessy. Since November he had won at Leopardstown, had won the Thyestes Chase at Gowran Park, and in February had lifted the Leopardstown Chase by twelve lengths under 12 stone. Arkle had not stood still since the Hennessy.

Willie Robinson jumped off quickly with Mill House and set a swinging gallop, jumping with an effortless rhythm, while Pat Taaffe was restraining Arkle, who was pulling hard for his head. Is there, I wonder, a finer sight than a lovely big chaser jumping boldly, being ridden by a horseman of William Robinson's style and poise? It all looked so easy, and Mill House was jumping an exhibition round, but the worrying time for his supporters came at the top of the hill when it was clear that no matter how well Mill House was jumping, Arkle seemed tied to his tail. Robinson now tried desperate measures to rid himself of the ominous shadow behind. He raced Mill House down the hill and rousted him into the third-last fence as if it was not there, but it was to no avail; Arkle remained on station, poised like a panther ready to strike.

The crunch came on the last bend when Robinson went for his whip and found it spinning out of his grasp. At that same moment Pat Taaffe, with singularly little subtlety, set Arkle in motion and they simply ran round Mill House like a wing three-quarter runs round a wrong-footed full-back. Arkle now showed British racegoers the sight that for the next three years they were going to have to get used to: Arkle, head erect, ears pricked, sprinting home at the end of a fast-run race. Arkle beat Mill House by five lengths, and lowered the course record by 4 seconds. He was the master, and everyone who saw what he did to Mill House that day knew that they had seen a true champion.

It was quite magnificent, and it was the stuff that National Hunt racing enthusiasts, English and Irish, enjoy with uninhibited pleasure. I remember wondering on the way home whether I had done justice to a day which really deserved the attentions of the Poet Laureate.

CHELTENHAM, Thur., Mar. 7th 1964
GOLD CUP (Chase) £8,004 3m 2f 130yds 3.50

ARKLE 7–12–0	PTaaffe	–1
Mill House 7–12–0	GWRobinson	5.2
Pas Seul 11–12–0	DDick	25.3
King's Nephew 10–12–0	SMellor	15.4

S.P.: 8/13 Mill House, 7/4 ARKLE, 20/1 King's Nephew, 50/1 Pas Seul. (Anne, Duchess of Westminster) T. Dreaper, Ireland. 4 Rn 6m 45.3

1965
Grand National

Jay Trump and Freddie

In 1965 the BBC Television features producer Anthony de Lotbinière dreamed up the idea of filming the favourite for the Grand National in the weeks leading up to the big race, covering every aspect of training and the people connected with the horse, as well as the betting market. He enlisted my help in deciding which horses to go for and to make the contacts and arrangements for filming. My advice was to film two horses – Freddie, the favourite, and also the American chaser Jay Trump who had won the Maryland Hunt Cup twice and was now with Fred Winter to be trained for the National.

So for three weeks a film crew dogged the footsteps of Jay Trump at Lambourn and Freddie, miles away at the home of Betty and Reg Tweedie at Gordon near Kelso. The most friendly co-operation was given by both trainers and this resulted in some quite remarkable footage of film being shot of the work behind the scenes leading up to Aintree. Then a crisis erupted at Lambourn when it appeared that Fred Winter's horses were stricken with a virus. Jay Trump and his American amateur rider Tommy Smith were isolated in another part of the village, even the trainer kept away and cameramen were banned.

At this stage we received permission from Clarence House to film the Queen Mother's chaser The Rip at Peter Cazalet's stable at Fairlawne in Kent.

Up in Scotland the Tweedies were exceptionally kind to the film crew, who obtained some most attractive shots of Freddie and Reg Tweedie rounding up the sheep. All was going well when the crew followed the Tweedies' horse box from Kelso to Aintree. Once there, however, the camera crew most unfortunately offended the then Aintree Clerk of the Course, James Bidwell-Topham. A very worried Anthony de Lotbinière sought me out to tell me that his crew had been banned from entering Aintree racecourse.

This was indeed a setback, and so I went into Paddock Lodge and spent a diplomatic tea-time with Mrs Topham and explained to her the significance of the film in relation to the future of the Grand National, and the marvellous publicity it would bring by being on BBC Television. While this was going on, Anthony de Lotbinière was pacing up and down outside, thinking that the work of the last three weeks had been wasted. Finally Mrs Topham relented and allowed them to film on the course, and Lord Sefton even gave permission to film inside the weighing room.

The Race

Freddie was the 7 to 2 favourite for the 1965 Grand National, and there were forty-seven runners. There had also been forty-seven in 1963 and 1966 and in Teal's year of 1952; in Freebooter's year (1950) there had been forty-nine. When Caughoo had come through the fog in 1947 to win by twenty lengths there had been no fewer than fifty-seven starters, seventeen more than the present safety limit of forty. This was my fifth Grand National for BBC Radio and it produced the most memorable finish between two extremely courageous chasers, one American-bred, the other Irish-bred but trained in Scotland.

There was no doubt about Freddie's stamina, and Pat McCarron had him in the leading five on the first circuit. At the water jump Rondetto led from Peacetown, the French challenger L'Empereur, Kapeno and Freddie. Following Fred Winter's instructions to the letter Tommy Smith had Jay Trump in twelfth place, but he began to move up as they ran towards Bechers for the second time. Here Kapeno fell when going well, just as he was to do in 1966. Rondetto was still going strongly in the lead when he fell at the twenty-sixth fence, and this left Freddie in front of Jay Trump, Vultrix, Mr Jones, Rainbow Battle and The Rip.

Now Jay Trump on the inside and Freddie drew clear of the pursuing pack. Freddie was staying on and so they jumped the last two fences, but Jay Trump was just the quicker away from them. On the long run-in the American horse looked as if he had Freddie beaten. But then the Scottish chaser showed his true mettle and slowly he began to draw up to Jay Trump. It was raw courage, and Pat McCarron asked Freddie to call on all his reserves of strength and stamina; but this last-ditch effort simply galvanised Tommy Smith – he had not travelled across the world to be denied now.

Fred Winter and Reg Tweedie, the two trainers involved watching from different parts of the Grandstand, were willing their respective jockeys to put down their whips. Almost by magic Tommy Smith seemed to receive this piece of telepathy and it won him the race, for Jay Trump answered the final call and held on by a diminishing three-quarters of a length.

It would have been a marvellous result whichever horse had won, and it was a pity there had to be a loser. The lean and hungry Tommy Smith had dreamed of winning the Grand National while he had been rising to the top of the steeplechasing tree in Maryland, and having won two Hunt Cups there, he had brought this tough horse over to realise his life's ambition. In the long history of the National I doubt if there has ever been such a remarkable story of single-minded dedication and professional application. Fred Winter just could not believe how anyone with such limited experience of English racing could do it. Tommy Smith had ridden in only four previous races and had never even seen Aintree except in photographs. Jay Trump had given Fred his very first win as a trainer back in October 1964 and had now provided his first Grand National win with his first runner in the race.

I felt enormous sympathy for the Tweedies – they represent the very best there is in National Hunt racing – but the hoodoo on Scottish-trained horses in the National continued. In the runner-up berth at Aintree there is a plaque commemorating the historic achievement of Macmoffat, who finished second in 1939 and 1940. Wyndburgh was runner-up twice and third once. But it was not until 1979 that Rubstic became the first ever Scottish-trained winner. Anthony de Lotbinière was beside himself as he directed the filming of the scenes after the race. 'We have ourselves a very considerable scoop; first and second, what a marvellous result.' When the film *The Favourite* was televised some three weeks later it received a tremendous reception. Inevitably I was asked afterwards whether the BBC had filmed *all* the horses beforehand. No one believed that we had filmed just the first two and The Rip, who finished seventh.

After it was all over Anthony de Lotbinière wrote a letter to my then chief, Mr Charles Max Muller, and kindly sent a copy to me. When things start looking black I have been knownto take it out and read it again – it was that kind of letter.

Freddie had been bought in Ireland with the National in mind on the advice of Stewart Wight, the trainer and life-long friend of Reg Tweedie. In that long drawn-out duel Freddie had quite literally run his heart out. The following year he returned to Aintree and was second again, beaten once more by a horse trained by Fred Winter, Anglo.

In the 1966/7 season Freddie was running well, winning four times including the Gallagher Gold Cup at Sandown, so hopes were high for the third time even though he had to carry 11 stone 13 lb in the 1967 National. At the pile-up at the twenty-third fence, like most of the field Freddie was baulked, though he eventually scrambled over to finish seventeenth. The following season Reg Tweedie retired his old friend as Freddie had begun to show traces of a heart murmur, incurred originally perhaps in that 1965 National.

Reg Tweedie was a great cross-country rider himself. He rode as an amateur from 1932 to 1949, and in 1940 he had finished fifth in the Grand National on Venturesome Knight, despite breaking a blood vessel in the year that Bogscar had beaten Macmoffat. I know that he would dearly have loved to have taken the trophy back to Kelso.

Freddie enjoyed a long and happy retirement on the farm. In his later years he had the companionship of Betty Tweedie's remarkable brood mare Rosie Wings, who produced thirteen foals, the majority of them winners, including Mount Athos who finished third in the Derby. When Freddie died in 1985 at the age of twenty-eight, from a heart attack, Rosie Wings would not leave him and broke away from the groom to return to her constant companion. She was inconsolable and in the end, much to everyone's distress, she had to be put down. She was the same age as Freddie. It was a double loss for the Tweedies, who loved their horses – they were part of the family – and rather in the style of Captain Ryan Price of Findon, they saw that their old friends enjoyed the happy retirement that they had so richly deserved.

LIVERPOOL, Sat., Mar. 27th 1965
GRAND NATIONAL CHASE (H'cap) £22,041
4m 856yds 3.15

JAY TRUMP 8–11–5	MrCSmith	–1
Freddie 8–11–10	PMcCarron	¾.2
Mr Jones 10–11–5	MrCCollins	20.3
Rainbow Battle 9–10–13	GMilburn	1.4
Vultrix 7–11–1	DNicholson	12.5
L'Empereur 11–10–13	MrJCiechanowski	12.6
The Rip 10–11–5	WRees	7
Loving Record 11–11–0	BHannon	8
TantPis 10–10–13	Mr JAlder	9
Brown Diamond 10–10–13	MrWMcLernon	10
April Rose 10–10–13	MajPBengough	11
Culleenhouse 11–10–13	TBiddlecombe	12

S.P.: 7/2 Freddie, 9/1 The Rip, 100/8 Rondetto, Kapeno, 100/6 JAY TRUMP, Vultrix, 18/1 Leeds, 22/1 Forgotten Dreams, 25/1 Culleenhouse, Peacetown, Quintin Bay, 33/1 Red Tide, Loving Record, Leslie, Phebu, Ruby Glen, 40/1 Time, TantPis, Reproduction, 50/1 Brown Diamond, Vulcano, Cutlette, Pontin-Go, Rainbow Battle, Mr Jones, Ayala. (Mrs M. Stephenson) F. T. Winter, Lambourn. 47 Rn 9m 31.80

1965
Derby

Sea Bird

Psidium's Derby in 1961 had been my first commentary for BBC Radio from the Grandstand at Epsom. The 66 to 1 unconsidered winner had come from last to first in a dramatic dash on the outside of the field. Then came the multiple fall in 1962 when Larkspur survived the pile-up on Tattenham Hill. Relko and the subsequent doping enquiry followed, and there was again plenty of animosity when Santa Claus won in 1964. For my fifth Derby hardly anything happened to raise the blood pressure, for Sea Bird II was quite the easiest winner in the long history of the race, until Shergar.

Trained by Etienne Pollet, Sea Bird II had just one season of glory. Though twice successful over seven furlongs as a two-year-old in France, he was rather overshadowed by his stablemate, the brilliant Grey Dawn II, who won three of France's four top two-year-old races, the Prix Morny, the Prix de la Salamandre and the Gran Criterium. Sea Bird II, very much the second string, had finished two lengths second in the Gran Criterium but he was running on at the finish and was bred to stay. He became the stable's Derby hope, with Grey Dawn II reserved for the French equivalent of the Two Thousand Guineas.

Pollet, the tall, immaculately dressed trainer, was one of the most respected members of his profession and was never afraid to travel his horses to Britain when they were good enough. He had sent Thunderhead II to capture the 1952 Two Thousand Guineas; the following year Pan II won the Gold Cup; in 1960 Never Too Late won both the One Thousand Guineas and the Oaks; and three years later Hula Dancer plundered both the One Thousand Guineas and the Champion Stakes. Pollet had exercised a remarkable hold on the top two-year-old races and Grey Dawn II was following in the footsteps of Hula Dancer and Right Royal, who had both won the Salamandre and the Criterium.

On the strength of the Gran Criterium form, Grey Dawn II was placed top of the French Free Handicap with 9 stone 6 lb, and Sea Bird three pounds lower with 9.3. On this occasion, however, two-year-old form proved an unreliable guide, for as three-year-olds Grey Dawn II was a failure and was exported to the USA while Sea Bird II became European champion.

After Sea Bird II had galloped away with the Prix Greffulhe and the far more prestigious Prix Lupin, Etienne Pollet announced that the next stop would be Epsom. Such had been the impact of winning the Lupin, as well as Pollet's reputation as a master of his craft, that Sea Bird II was immediately named favourite for the Derby. At that time the French three-year-olds were dominant, and two exceptional horses, Reliance II and Diatome, were to contest the Prix du Jockey Club (the French equivalent of the Derby).

The Race

On Derby day Sea Bird opened up at 11 to 4, even though few had seen him in action; sheer weight of money forced the price down to 7 to 4 at the off. The British-trained three-year-olds were a weak bunch, with the Two Thousand Guineas winner Niksar and Gulf Pearl, successful in the Chester Vase, the best we could muster. Paddy Prendergast had engaged Lester Piggott to ride Meadow Court, one of whose owners was Bing Crosby. The Australian jockey Pat Glennon was riding Sea Bird II. The 66 to 1 outsider Sunaccelli led at Tattenham Corner, until I Say (carrying the same colours as Reference Point) burst into a clear lead. Sea Bird was now making up his ground steadily and in a few strides he took I Say as if he were standing still, and went clear. Though Meadow Court stayed on well to be second, the fact is that Sea Bird won in a common canter. I was practically speechless, for I had never imagined that a Derby could be won in such a ridiculously easy manner – which posed the question, is Sea Bird that good, or are the others so bad?

Meadow Court answered that question quite soon for, again ridden by Lester Piggott, he won the Irish Sweeps Derby and then the King George VI and Queen Elizabeth Stakes. I Say became an imposing four-year-old and won the Coronation Cup. Sea Bird himself went from strength to strength, missing the King George and running instead in the Grand Prix de Saint Cloud, where he beat older horses in much the same way as his win in the Derby.

Whenever a top international horse, such as Nijinsky, Mill Reef or Dancing Brave, arrives on the scene, the first consideration is how he compares with Sea Bird II. It is difficult to see just why Sea Bird II was so superior to the rest of his generation. He was not particularly distinguished in looks, being a tall, rather rangy chestnut with two white socks behind; he did not initially impress by his appearance at Epsom. But when he was seen in action, he moved with a silk-like, athletic grace. Anyone who had not seen him before he ran in the Derby would have been won over simply by watching him move to the post.

His pedigree was uninspiring: he was by Dan Cupid, the first crop of the great American sire Native Dancer, but the bottom line showed that not one of his five female antecedents had won a race of any description. He could have been picked up for a song had he been offered at auction, going strictly on the catalogue. What Sea Bird II clearly needed was time, and with the Master Pollet that was what he was given. He was at his peak for the Arc, but what a shame he did not stay in training as a four-year-old.

Sea Bird II ran for the last time in the Prix de l'Arc de Triomphe, where he met the winner and the runner-up in the Prix du Jockey Club, Reliance II and Diatome. It was another superb performance, and he beat them by six lengths and five lengths despite swerving out left into the centre of the course. Racing journalist Tom Nickalls wrote in the *Sporting Life:* 'The sight of Sea Bird outclassing nineteen opponents in the Prix de l'Arc de Triomphe was something quite out of this world.'

The Jockey Club handicapper alloted Sea Bird II 10.2 in the three-year-old Free Handicap, placing him 14 lb above Meadow Court, while *Timeform* gave Sea Bird II a rating of 145 – the highest ever accorded to any horse since that organisation had begun assessing racehorses twenty years earlier. By comparison, Ribot had been rated at 142 in 1952.

Sea Bird II went off to stud in the USA immediately after the Arc. He was leased for five years to a syndicate of American breeders headed by Mr John Galbraith, to stand at his Derby Dan Stud alongside Ribot. He was not the success that had been expected at stud, however, and he returned to France in 1973, but died shortly afterwards. His best son proved to be Gyr, who had the bad luck to be born in the same year as Nijinsky.

EPSOM, Wed., Jun. 2nd 1965
DERBY STAKES £65,301 1m 4f 3.30

SEA BIRD II 9–0	TGlennon	–1
Meadow Court 9–0	LPiggott	2.2
I Say 9–0	RPoincelet	1½.3
Niksar 9–0	WRickaby	4.4
Convamore 9–0	EHide	½.5
Cambridge 9–0	ABreasley	1.6

S.P.: 7/4 SEA BIRD II, 10/1 Meadow Court, 100/8 Niksar, Gulf Pearl, 20/1 Foothill, 25/1 Look Sharp, Cambridge, Alcalde, Ballymarais, Vleuten, 28/1 I Say, 33/1 As Before. (M. J. Ternynck) E. Pollet, France. 22 Rn 2m 38.41

1970
Prix de l'Arc de Triomphe

Sassafras and Nijinsky

1970 was the year of Nijinsky, a Canadian-bred colt who, in the two years that he raced in Britain, captured the interest and the imagination of the racing public. After winning the Dewhurst Stakes as a two-year-old, he went into winter quarters unbeaten and favourite for the Two Thousand Guineas and the Derby. Nijinsky looked every inch a champion. He was a big colt and he moved with a grace and majesty that were breathtaking – and for such an imposing individual he had a lot of speed. We are always seeking the 'wonder horse' and here, it seemed, was exactly that.

Nijinsky had been bought at the Woodbine Sales in Toronto on Vincent O'Brien's advice by Mr Charles Engelhard, one of the world's richest men, whose wealth derived from the family holding in the company Engelhard Hanovia, which had extensive mining interests around the world. Engelhard, known as the 'Platinum King', maintained nine homes around the world, and was an international sportsman with an overriding passion for horse racing. He already had stables in America and South Africa, and a chance meeting with David McCall, then of the London Bloodstock Agency, started in a small way in Britain what was later to become a racing empire on a global scale.

Following the modest purchase of a four-year-old mare, Ticklish, in 1959, David McCall bought the Ribot colt Romulus, who became a top-class miler. This initiated Mr Engelhard's interest in Ribot's offspring. The first Classic winner in the green, red and yellow colours was Indiana who, after finishing second to Santa Claus in the Derby, won the St Leger ridden by Jimmy Lindley. The brothers Ribocco and Ribero both won the Irish Sweeps Derby and the St Leger, an exceptional feat of training by Fulke Johnson Houghton. However, the other side of the coin was also experienced by Mr Engelhard when another Ribot colt, Ribofilio, proved a total failure in the Two Thousand Guineas. Ribofilio trailed in last at Newmarket, and though the dope test proved negative, no explanation has ever been forthcoming for his poor running, which baffled the vets, stunned the punters and in the press raised the spectre of foul play.

Sadly, Nijinsky was to prove Mr Engelhard's 'swan song', for by 1970 he was a very sick man, suffering considerable pain from an arthritic hip. I always felt that there were two important factors in the success of Nijinsky: firstly, that no one deserved to own a horse of this calibre more than Charles Engelhard; and secondly, that it was very fortunate that Vincent O'Brien was his handler, for training this particular son of Northern Dancer proved to be no sinecure.

Nijinsky came most impressively through his Guineas preparation race, the Gladness Stakes at the Curragh, and at Newmarket for the Two Thousand Guineas he was 7 to 4 on.

I always try to view a big race field in the pre-parade ring while the previous race is being run – with a big crowd there is always a risk that you might become trapped and not return to the roof in time. I was unable on this occasion to get to see Nijinsky, for he was kept out of sight until the last minute in the brick saddling yard and the press of people made it unlikely that many would see him even in the parade ring. I therefore rely on the concise and authoritative description in *Timeform*'s 'Racehorses of 1970':

In the paddock before the Two Thousand Guineas Nijinsky outclassed his rivals in appearance as seldom a classic field can have been outclassed before. He moved down to the start majestically, and his performance in the race itself was worthy of a Classic.

Lester Piggott rode with the utmost confidence, a style that was to succeed again in the Derby. Here the French colt Gyr, a massive chestnut and a difficult ride, was handled with consummate skill round Tattenham Corner by Bill Williamson, and he got first run in the straight. Gyr, well as he ran, was just the aiming mark that Nijinsky needed, and Lester swooped to conquer in the last furlong.

The last few days before the Derby had been worrying for Vincent O'Brien and his travelling head lad Gerry Gallagher, for Nijinsky had had a bout of colic on the Monday before the event and with the race only forty-eight hours away he could not be given any medication. This was a crisis of enormous proportions, and Vincent O'Brien telephoned David McCall and asked him to inform Charles Engelhard, who was in London, that it was now unlikely that the horse could run. David McCall considered the implications, and was concerned as to how this shattering news would be received by Nijinsky's owner.

It was now mid-day, and David McCall swallowed a large vodka and went round to Charles Engelhard's offices in Grosvenor Square, dreading the next few minutes. David entered the office and asked to see his boss, but the secretary said, 'Oh, you must have passed him in the lift, he has gone to the City and will not be back until later this afternoon.' With a sense of relief that the bad news had at least been delayed, he returned to his office.

Later in the afternoon Vincent O'Brien telephoned again with better news of Nijinsky – the spasm had passed and the horse was now all right and would run. David McCall decided against telling Charles Engelhard, and indeed it was not until the morning after Nijinsky had won the Derby, when they were both still suffering from hangovers from the previous night's celebrations, that he spilt the beans. Engelhard surprised David by saying, 'Well, I knew something was wrong. I just had a gut feeling about it.'

On Derby day few people knew about Nijinsky's problems, but Lester Piggott realised that the horse was not one hundred per cent and he asked the colt only to do enough to win. He did, by two and a half lengths. It had looked smooth and easy, and the impression that here indeed was a wonder horse was confirmed. Everyone awaited with eager anticipation Nijinsky's next appearance against the older horses in the King George VI and Queen Elizabeth Stakes at Ascot.

Before that, Nijinsky was 'at home' in front of a huge crowd at the Curragh for the Irish Sweeps Derby, where he was ridden by the stable's retained jockey in Ireland, Liam Ward. Although he became upset during the preliminaries, Nijinsky won readily, beating Meadowville by three lengths.

At Ascot in the King George VI and Queen Elizabeth Stakes, Nijinsky was the only three-year-old in the field. This time I did get to see him under the leafy trees in the top paddock by the saddling boxes. I was enthralled – he was in magnificent shape and had become quite the best-looking horse I can remember. On that warm, sunny day his coat gleamed, he was on good terms with himself; I wished that I could have filmed him walking round the paddock like a king. But handsome is as handsome does, and he was soon to live up to those good looks with a breathtaking performance in the race. Lester produced him almost nonchalantly to challenge the previous year's Derby winner Blakeney, and then in a few strides it was all over and Lester eased Nijinsky back before the post so that the winning margin between him and Blakeney was down to two lengths.

Nijinsky was now unbeaten in ten races. He had beaten the older generation and was now hot stallion property – where to now? The answer to that question, it soon transpired, was going to depend on the veterinary surgeons, not the trainer, for after his most glorious moment and while at the pinnacle of his career, Nijinsky fell ill. Within a week of his return to Ballydoyle he contracted a severe attack of ringworm, and was soon to lose most of the hair on one side. He could not be saddled, so he could not be ridden out. This was a frustrating time for Vincent O'Brien, for Charles Engelhard had set his heart on winning the Triple Crown and with two English Classics already in the bag the St Leger seemed to be there for the taking.

The vets won the race for time, and Vincent decided on tackling the St Leger on the way to the colt's prime autumn objective, the Prix de l'Arc de Triomphe. Before the Derby there had been questions as to Nijinsky's ability to stay a mile and a half. These were now revived.

In the St Leger Lester Piggott, his mind clearly set on the Arc, rode an absolutely masterly race to win. He had the race won a long way out, and he just kept Nijinsky going strongly enough to keep Meadowville at bay by merely a length, with Lester looking round constantly in the last furlong.

Nijinsky therefore became the first horse since the Aga Khan's Bahram in 1935 to win the Triple Crown. Post-war history was made that afternoon, and Charles Engelhard became so overcome with emotion in the unsaddling enclosure that he had to be helped away. I found him sitting in his Rolls Royce in the car park, his collar undone, drinking a Coke from the can. With tears rolling down his face he said, 'This is the happiest moment of my life.' I remember thinking at the time that owning a superhorse ought to carry a Government health warning!

Vincent O'Brien had achieved what a month earlier had appeared to be impossible. The colt seemed to have had an easy race, so I was surprised to read in Ivor Herbert's book *Vincent O'Brien's Great Horses* that Nijinsky had returned home 29 lb lighter, suggesting that the toll of travelling to contest these races had been as great as the races themselves. With hindsight, Vincent told Ivor that the St Leger would have been prejudicial to his Arc preparation. Perhaps I should have used the St Leger when Nijinsky made history, or the King George when he was at his peak, for my most memorable race. It will probably remain the only Triple Crown that I will ever describe, for the experience of Nijinsky and later Reference Point suggests that the St Leger is run too close to the Arc. No three-year-old has ever won both races.

The Race

So Nijinsky went to the Arc with an unbeaten and unblemished record. He was now worth a fortune as a stallion, but the Arc would just put the gilt on his portfolio. He had beaten older horses once in the King George, but for international breeders the Arc was the jackpot. It seemed inconceivable that he could be beaten.

It may seem churlish to include Nijinsky's first defeat in this almanac of memorable races, but in all the years that I have had the privilege of describing great and momentous happenings in mere words, this particular Arc was the most dramatic, the most tragic and the saddest of all. Up until this time Lester Piggott's Arc record had not been good: he had been beaten into second place on Park Top the previous year and in 1968 had again been runner-up on Sir Ivor; in 1967 he had finished third on Ribocco.

In 1969, before going out to ride Park Top, Lester had ridden the winners of the three previous races on Tower Walk, Shaft and Vela. While Bill Williamson was waiting in the weighing room to give the saddle for Levmoss to the trainer, Seamus McGrath, I suggested to him that with Lester in such form it did not seem worth bothering to take part. With a wry smile 'Weary Willie', as he was affectionately known, drawled, 'I think that he may just have used up all his luck.' Bill was right, for he got first run on Levmoss, who had won the Gold Cup, and Lester's late challenge on Park Top failed by three-quarters of a length.

In their superb essay on Nijinsky, *Timeform*'s 'Racehorses of 1970' posed the question: 'Did Sassafras win the Arc or did Nijinsky lose it?' Certainly, no race that I can remember caused so much post-race controversy. This was to be Nijinsky's last race and Vincent O'Brien, while admiring the confident way in which Lester Piggott had ridden the colt in all his victories so far, attempted to sow seeds in Lester's mind that for a race like the Arc it was essential to lie up closer to the pace than he had in his previous races. When Vincent telephoned Lester to inform him of Nijinsky's progress after the St Leger, Ivor Herbert wrote, 'Lester replied that he wouldn't mind if he had a hundred horses in front of him.'

Nijinsky Beaten Sensation

Up to around 4.25 p.m. on that Arc day, Nijinsky was being heralded as the best horse since Sea Bird II, maybe even better, for Sea Bird II had not won the Triple Crown even though he had won the Derby and the Arc by wide margins. Nijinsky had won all his races with the utmost authority and only Lester's restraint had prevented him from winning by spectacular distances. Nijinsky was unbeaten, whereas Sea Bird II had finished second in the Gran Criterium as a two-year-old.

The atmosphere at Longchamp was electric, and as usual there was a huge contingent of British and Irish racegoers present at this superbly staged meeting. In the paddock Nijinsky looked majestic, but the authorities were guilty of a total dereliction of their responsibility in allowing a horde of unruly cameramen into the parade ring, where the 'rat pack' pursued and harried Nijinsky from the moment he entered until he left the ring. As a two-year-old Nijinsky had showed signs of nerves, and he was a much more highly strung individual than any of us realised. Before the Irish Sweeps Derby the enormous crowd had unsettled him and he had sweated up profusely. It did not seem to affect his running on that occasion, for he won impressively, but an over-excited horse before the race is not always easy to control during it. Nijinsky left the paddock and went out on to the course edgy and sweating.

The Derby runner-up, Gyr, and the Italian Derby winner, Ortis, both had pacemakers in Golden Eagle and Lar, and they made the early running with the French St Leger winner Sassafras always just third or fourth. Ortis and Blakeney came next, with Gyr awash with sweat giving Bill Williamson a miserable ride. At the top of the hill Nijinsky had only five runners behind him, but now he began to close. Miss Dan led from Ortis, then came

Sassafras, Gyr and Blakeney and Lester still making ground on Nijinsky. Two furlongs from the finish Sassafras moved into the lead travelling strongly. Lester, attempting to get through the pack to challenge, now found his way blocked with little hope of a gap appearing. He was therefore forced wide, and this not entirely unexpected traffic problem, so often a feature of the Arc, meant that he had given Sassafras about ten lengths' start.

Nijinsky, now under the strongest driving that he had ever experienced, made up the leeway showing a magnificent surge of speed, but he was under pressure to make this challenge. He left all his rivals behind, but Sassafras was not flinching – he was, after all, a staying horse, stoutly bred – and yet Nijinsky's long run through the field carried him level. My radio commentary position at Longchamp is high but about a hundred yards short of the winning line. I am still certain that Nijinsky got his head in front, but by now they were racing away from me and widely separated. What happened in the dying seconds of this most dramatic race has become the greatest source of argument and debate in racing.

So, did Sassafras win the Arc, or did Nijinsky lose it? There is no doubt in my mind that Nijinsky lost it. The prodigious effort made by Piggott to make up so much ground, and the extra distance he travelled in order to find his opening, left Nijinsky with no reserve, and having so bravely got to a challenging position his stamina ran out and he swerved away to the left.

The rider of Sassafras was Yves St Martin, the greatest jockey that France has produced, and in a flash he instinctively realised that Nijinsky was in trouble and reacted by riding the brave stayer under him with a demon-like ferocity which carried him on relentlessly to the post. From my position I was not sure which horse had won, but I feared that Nijinsky had been beaten and said so. It took some saying, for I felt the most bitter and abject disappointment that this great colt's colours had been lowered.

The villain Yves St Martin and Sassafras had spoilt the story. How dare they ruin my day and crush the spirits of all the Irish present? And who the hell was Sassafras anyway – he had won the French St Leger only on an objection – and what right had he to beat the greatest horse we had seen since the war? Those were the thoughts going through my head when the result of the photograph was announced – Sassafras the winner by a head. This wholly biased view was shared by many racegoers, so that the credit due to Sassafras was never properly accorded. Our thoughts were all on Nijinsky.

After the race Lester Piggott was criticised by Vincent O'Brien for over-confidence by giving Nijinsky so much ground to make up. Lester countered this by saying that the horse never gave him the same feel. 'He had lost his fire', was the way that he put it. There had been no change in tactics, he had ridden Nijinsky in just the same way to eleven previous victories. In those last dreadful yards, the four journeys to Britain and one to France had taken their toll; the attentions of the posse of cameramen had not helped; and then, for once, Lester had not enjoyed the luck in running.

Charles Engelhard took it badly; he was very emotionally involved with all his horses and particularly Nijinsky, and after the race he was beyond the consolation of his friends. Remembering the unfortunate experience that had befallen Ribocco in the Arc when he had finished like a train and just failed to catch the outsider Topyo, David McCall had been anxious lest a similar fate might befall Nijinsky and that Lester would be boxed in and lose the race. For the health of his owner, that was a nightmare that he had hoped would not happen.

The party arranged in case Nijinsky won had been cancelled, and the next day David McCall visited Charles Engelhard who was still in bed, still distressed and in tears. They discussed plans for Nijinsky. David McCall was insistent that they should call it a day and not run him in the Champion Stakes. They discussed the horse's future at stud, and the gloom receded when Mr Engelhard said that the thing to which he was now most looking forward was seeing Nijinsky's first foals. This he was never able to do, for that meeting was the last time that David saw his owner alive. The following March Charles Engelhard died of a heart attack at the age of fifty-four, in his winter home at Boca Grande in Florida. As David McCall put it: 'English racing has lost a great supporter and myself a personal friend.'

Sad to relate, Nijinsky did run in the Champion Stakes and was beaten by Lorenzaccio, which rather confirmed Lester Piggott's opinion that the horse was not the one he had ridden in the summer.

Nijinsky retired to Bull Hancock's Claiborne Farm in Kentucky with a price of five and half million dollars on his head. When I visited the stud in 1977 Nijinsky looked magnificent, and I feel that Charles Engelhard would have been proud of his outstanding record at stud: the sire of an English Derby winner, Golden Fleece; a Kentucky Derby winner, Ferdinand; and Ile De Bourbon, winner of the King George VI and Queen Elizabeth Stakes.

LONGCHAMP, Sun., Oct. 4th (Good)
PRIX DE L'ARC DE TRIOMPHE £103,744 1m 4f

SASSAFRAS 3–8–10	YSaint-Martin	–1
Nijinsky (CAN) 3–8–10	LPiggott	hd.2
Miss Dan 3–8–7	JTaillard	2.3
Gyr (USA) 3–8–10	WWilliamson	1½.4
Blakeney 4–9–6	ABarclay	1½.5
Beaugency (FR) 4–9–6	FHead	s.hd.6
Soyeux 5–9–6	SLeonardos	2.7
Quinquet 4–9–6	YJosse	¾.8
Grandier 6–9–6	MPhillipperon	4.9
Chara 4–9–6	ALequeux	nk.10

S.P.: 4/10 Nijinsky, 19/1 Sassafras, 38/1 Miss Dan (Arpad Plesch) F. Mathet, France. 15 Rn 2m 29.70

1971
Two Thousand Guineas

Brigadier Gerard

The build-up for the Two Thousand Guineas of 1971 had begun in the autumn of the previous year, for it was apparent that in My Swallow and Mill Reef we had two quite outstanding colts of Classic calibre; their target was to be the first colts' Classic.

My Swallow, owned by the philanthropist Mr David Robinson, had become the first horse ever to complete the 'grand slam' in the Group 1 two-year-old races in France, namely the Prix Morny, the Prix Robert Papin, the Prix de la Salamandre and the Gran Criterium. My Swallow had headed the French equivalent of the Free Handicap, and although this strapping colt had run only twice in England, winning a minor race at York and the Woodcote Stakes at Epsom, he had been placed top of the English Free Handicap too.

Mill Reef, owned and bred by Mr Paul Mellon, had also proved a top two-year-old, winning the Coventry Stakes, the Imperial Stakes, the Gimcrack and the Dewhurst. His only defeat had come when he had travelled to France to take on My Swallow in the Prix Robert Papin, when he was beaten by a short head. In compiling their handicaps the French and English officials used that race to assess the merit of both colts, placing My Swallow one pound above Mill Reef.

Brigadier Gerard, bred and owned by John Hislop, the outstanding amateur rider of his generation, was unbeaten in four races as a two-year-old. Although on paper he had not achieved as much as the other two colts, he had ended his season by winning the Middle Park Stakes in tremendous style. The handicapper rated him 9 stone 5 lb in the

Free Handicap, one pound below Mill Reef and two pounds below My Swallow.

The first appearance of these colts was eagerly awaited. My Swallow was due to contest the Kempton Trial, and Mill Reef the Greenham at Newbury. Brigadier Gerard's connections did not wish to take on either of these colts until the Guineas. John Hislop describes in his book *The Brigadier* that he did not wish to give weight away in the Craven Stakes, and the other trial at Thirsk entailed a long journey, so he decided to run Brigadier Gerard in the Two Thousand Guineas without a previous race.

My Swallow, in magnificent shape, came out and won the Usher Stakes over seven furlongs at Kempton against minor opposition. Mill Reef, looking fit and well, simply ran away with the Greenham. Out of sight and out of mind, Dick Hern was bringing Brigadier Gerard to peak fitness at home at West Ilsley.

Racing memories are short. The late Sir Noel Murless had sent out Crepello and Royal Palace to win the Two Thousand Guineas without a previous race, but I and most of my colleagues had, I suspect, become mesmerised into thinking that the Guineas was a two-horse race between the top two colts in the Free Handicap. On the day before the Guineas John Hislop had gone out of his way to inform me of the Brigadier's progress at home and how he had 'cleared out' older horses such as Richboy and Duration. Clearly Brigadier Gerard had 'trained on', and John Hislop discounted the literal interpretation of the Greenham running of Swing Easy, beaten by seven lengths by Mill Reef compared to the three and a half lengths by which the Brigadier had beaten the same horse in the Middle Park, reasoning that he did not consider that Swing Easy had come to hand in time for the Newbury race. How right was that paddock judgement to prove.

So Two Thousand Guineas day came, and with it perfect weather and an enormous crowd of enthusiastic racegoers to see what I still consider the greatest race for the Two Thousand Guineas I have ever described. With three such outstanding colts there was the smallest field since 1888, when Ayrshire had beaten five opponents. Lester Piggott, who had partnered My Swallow in all his races as a two-year-old, was claimed for Vincent O'Brien's stable to ride Minsky; Frankie Durr was therefore on board My Swallow. The remaining runners were Good Bond, who had won the Ascot Two Thousand Guineas Trial, and the American-bred Indian Ruler ridden by Brian Taylor.

With only six runners, race-reading would not prove difficult – the test would be for my powers of description, for whoever won this outstanding contest would surely be the Racehorse of the Year (though, as it turned out, this was not to be the case). At that stage of the season the Two Thousand Guineas was the limit of my horizon.

In the event the race was easily described. As a two-year-old My Swallow had made the running for all his Group 1 wins, and the Rowley Mile seemed ideal for this powerful galloper with his raking stride. Frankie Durr, drawn on the outside of the six, led the field followed by Mill Reef, Minsky (blinkered for the first time), with Brigadier Gerard racing fourth on the stands side.

My Swallow, in spite of the small field, drifted towards the centre of the course and Mill Reef, tracking his path, went across with him. At the Bushes, that famous landmark three furlongs from home, Mill Reef went to challenge My Swallow and headed him, but racing close to the standside rails Joe Mercer now sent Brigadier Gerard up to challenge the pair who were locked together in the centre of the course. Just as Mill Reef appeared to have mastered My Swallow, Brigadier Gerard quickened and shot into the lead. He kept up his run right on to the post and won by three lengths, with Mill Reef beating My Swallow by three-quarters of a length.

It was truly sensational, and my immediate thought voiced in the heat of the moment was that while Brigadier Gerard was perfectly entitled to win, he was not expected to beat the two best horses in Europe by *three* lengths and to prove six pounds superior to the top pair in the Free Handicap.

The two-horse-race fraternity was inclined to blame Frankie Durr and Geoff Lewis for cutting each other's throat and handing the race to Joe Mercer. This accusation is not borne out by the time of the race, which equalled the standard time of 1 minute 39.2 on good going, a time which has been bettered by six subsequent winners of the Two Thousand Guineas. El Gran Senor and Shadeed covered the Rowley Mile in identical times of 1 minute 37.41 in winning their Classics in 1984 and 1985. I did not see Tudor Minstrel win the Guineas in 1947 but John Hislop maintains that this was the most impressive win in this Classic since that year, and I would not disagree.

Yet the promise of a tremendous head-to-head finish had not materialised, and with hindsight and with the knowledge of Mill Reef's subsequent career it does seem that we were in a way cheated of one of the great finishes in the history of racing. Brigadier Gerard won too far, and to this day Ian Balding believes that Mill Reef was not himself that day.

Ian's case rests on a visit that he and Mill Reef's owner, Mr Paul Mellon, made to the Links stables at noon on the morning of the Guineas. The owner saw a relaxed colt, his coat gleaming like mahogany, the very picture of health. The owner commented, 'He looks ready.'

Mill Reef travelled the short distance from the racecourse stables to the course in the horse box. As he was being unloaded another runner, the ill-tempered Minsky, was already walking around giving his handlers a difficult time, rearing and plunging and being very 'colty'. Ian's experienced men Bill Jennings and John Hallam quickly got Mill Reef out of the way, but when Ian Balding came to saddle Mill Reef the horse was clearly upset and edgy and he was sweating, which he had never done before; he looked drawn and taut and was in a foul mood – which was quite uncharacteristic.

Unfortunately, when they paraded in order according to the racecard numbers, Minsky was immediately in front of Mill Reef. Ian describes Mill Reef as sensitive, and clearly his proximity to the outrageous behaviour of Minsky affected him: he was just not the same horse that Ian had seen three hours earlier.

My Swallow was a confirmed front runner and he came from his outside draw and powered his way straight down the centre of the course. Ian Balding's instruction to Geoff Lewis was 'not to hang about'. So Ian was surprised that Mill Reef did not stick to his station from a No 1 draw on the standside rails. If he had done this Joe Mercer would not have known which of the two horses to track: My Swallow or Mill Reef.

Tactically the race was run to suit Brigadier Gerard, for when Geoff Lewis took up his station on My Swallow's quarters he and Frankie Durr played cat and mouse and so it was a muddled early pace. Going through both jockeys' minds, no doubt, was the fear that they might indeed cut each other's throat and not last home. In fact they erred towards setting too slow a pace, and this played right into the hands of Joe Mercer.

Postscript

After the race John Hislop, with commendable speed, outlined his plans for Brigadier Gerard. What we all hoped for was a re-match with Mill Reef, but when we learnt that the Brigadier would stick to a mile until the Champion Stakes and would not run in the Derby, such a meeting appeared unlikely. The Eclipse Stakes was a possibility, but Brigadier Gerard missed that race and Mill Reef won it in a new course record time. Sadly, the two horses were never to meet again.

Brigadier Gerard went on to a magnificent career, winning seventeen races from eighteen starts and amassing a total of £243,924. He never campaigned abroad, and his sole defeat came in the Benson and Hedges Gold Cup at York when he finished second to Roberto. His trainer, Major Dick Hern, gained the admiration of the entire racing world for the skill with which he handled this popular horse.

My Swallow, the record-breaking two-year-old, did not enhance his reputation at three and after his gruelling race in the Guineas he failed to win, but ran a highly creditable second, in the July Cup when he was beaten only half a length by Realm.

Of Mill Reef you will hear more in the following chapter.

Newmarket, Sat., May 1st 1971 (Good)
2,000 GUINEAS STAKES (Gr 1) £27,283.40 (£8,004.00: £3,902.00: £1,030.60) 1m 2.50

BRIGADIER GERARD 9–0	JMercer	–1
Mill Reef (USA) 9–0	GLewis	3.2
My Swallow 9–0	FDurr	¾.3
Minsky (CAN) 9–0	LPiggott	5.4
Indian Ruler (USA) 9–0	BTaylor	12.5
Good Bond 9–0	JLindley	1½.6

S.P.: 6/4 Mill Reef, 2/1 My Swallow, 11/2 BRIGADIER GERARD, 15/2 Minsky, 16/1 Good Bond, 100/1 Indian Ruler. (Mrs J. L. Hislop) W. Hern, West Ilsley. 6 Rn 1m 39.20

1971
Prix de l'Arc de Triomphe

Mill Reef

After Mill Reef's defeat by Brigadier Gerard in the Two Thousand Guineas, their paths went separate ways. Brigadier Gerard was kept to a mile and won the St James's Palace Stakes at Royal Ascot. Mill Reef became the third North American-bred colt to win the Derby in four years, quite a novelty then although a fairly regular occurrence now.

After the Derby Mill Reef went to Sandown where he lowered the course record in the Eclipse Stakes. Another magnificent victory in the King George and Queen Elizabeth Stakes followed, Mill Reef winning by six lengths, the longest margin by which the race had ever been won. (In 1973 the French-trained filly Dahlia also won by six lengths.)

Now Ian Balding began to dream about the Arc, and Mill Reef's programme was geared to the first week in October. First, though, the colt was to have a rest from hard training; Ian planned six weeks' rest and four weeks' build-up to the Arc. (John Oaksey wrote in *The Story of Mill Reef* that he thought that one advantage of the colt's defeat in the Two Thousand Guineas was that it removed any temptation to chase the Triple Crown and to go for the St Leger.) However, after Mill Reef's rest, and as September drew on, Ian Balding became uneasy at the way that his colt was working at home. This was the first signal that he was beginning to 'train off' after being on the go since the spring. His fast work became gradually less impressive.

Mill Reef had experienced a particularly traumatic journey to France as a two-year-old to contest the Prix

Robert Papin. Ian Balding considered that this had largely contributed to his short-head defeat there by My Swallow. He was determined that the same thing would not happen again, and made meticulous plans for shipping the colt to France. This entailed getting special permission from the American Air Force to fly Mill Reef out from their Greenham Common Air Base, situated just a few miles from the stables at Kingsclere. Permission eventually came from the Pentagon, and the travel arrangements were made.

These were particularly anxious days for the trainer, but at least the journey to France went without a hitch and in just two hours from leaving his stables, Mill Reef was cleared through customs at Le Bourget. From there it was a short distance to Lamorlaye near Chantilly, where he was to be stabled before the Arc. At Maisons-Laffitte the previous year, Mill Reef had refused to eat and had come back home 40 lb lighter; this time there were no such problems.

Ian Balding likens the atmosphere at Longchamp on that Arc day to a rugby International. President Pompidou was present and thousands of British racegoers had travelled over; many were congregated at the Pimms bar near the stable entrance. When Mill Reef made his entrance a cheer went up from his fan club. However, discerning paddock judges were concerned that Mill Reef had run up light and there was a fear that he had 'gone over the top'. He looked even smaller against the magnificent four-year-olds on parade. From my eyrie high in the Grandstand I am able to get only a bird's-eye view of the paddock, so this anxiety over Mill Reef had not reached me. On the way to the post Mill Reef swept all these worries aside, for he took a tremendous hold on the way to the start with his head stuck out in its usual position.

Ian Balding was far from gloomy, even though he realised that Mill Reef was not in the same superb condition that he had been in high summer; at least he had travelled well. Ian also harboured a secret. When Mill Reef and his travel companion Aldie had worked on virgin ground on the Saturday morning at Lamorlaye, Mill Reef had gone exceptionally well. After the gallop, inspection of the hoofprints had revealed the secret of Mill Reef's extraordinary ability. While the handicapper Aldie had dug deep into the new turf, there was no evidence that Mill Reef had galloped there at all, for he had made no impression on the grass: a phantom galloper of perfect action floating over the turf like a Will o' the Wisp.

Well drawn, Mill Reef was very keen in the first half mile, and at the top of the hill, about six furlongs from home, Geoff Lewis had him perfectly poised in sixth place and looking comfortable. Ossian and Ramsin had made the running at a furious pace, but the downhill run from six furlongs out to the three-furlong point is the most critical stage in the Arc. Geoff Lewis was hugging the rails and now the worst happened, as Ossian began to struggle to keep station in the lead. As Ossian dropped away Mill Reef did a neat side-step and moved outside him, but now he found still more traffic problems when the ominous figure of Lester Piggott loomed up on his outside on Hallez, effectively blocking Geoff's escape route round the outside of the field.

From the stands the leading bunch seemed so tightly packed that the only chance that Mill Reef appeared to hold was to challenge wide of the field. At this point Ian Balding completely lost sight of the black and gold colours of Mr Paul Mellon. Mill Reef seemed to have sunk without trace. Ian suffered a moment of abject panic; Geoff was boxed in and would not escape in time.

This was indeed a crisis moment for Geoff, who had now to hope and pray for a gap to materialise. In the last curve as the bend straightens out Mill Reef, railing like a well-trained greyhound, saw the gap between Ortis and Hallez and in a surge of acceleration he was through and running. Running to such purpose, like a pigeon released from a cage he soared away and put daylight between him and the hunting pack behind.

To show such finishing speed at the end of a fast-run race (no Arc until then had been run faster) is the hallmark of a class racehorse, and amid wild cheering Mill Reef on that magical day at Longchamp became the first British-trained Derby winner to win the Arc; sixteen years on, he still is.

Mill Reef ran the Arc course in 2 minutes 28.3 seconds. The following year San San equalled that record and in 1980 Detroit set up a new record in 2 minutes 28 seconds exactly, which stood until Dancing Brave shaded that time by three-tenths of a second in 1986, clocking 2 minutes 27.7.

LONGCHAMP, Sun., Oct. 3rd 1971 (Good)
PRIX DE L'ARC DE TRIMPHE (Gr 1) £105,199.25 1m 4f

MILL REEF (USA) 3–8–10	GLewis	–1
Pistol Packer 3–8–7	FHead	3.2
Cambrizzia 3–8–7	ABarclay	1½.3
Caro 4–9–6	JLindley	nk.4
Hallez 4–9–6	LPiggott	¾.5
Royalty 3–8–10	JMercer	½.6
Bourbon 3–8–10	YSaint-Martin	nk.7
Arlequino 3–8–10	JMassard	s.nk.8
One or All (USA) 5–9–6	WCarson	½.9
Irish Ball 3–8–10	WPyers	s.hd.10

S.P.: 7/10 Mill Reef, 17/40 Pistol Packer, Bourbon, 39/1 Cambrizzia.
(P. Mellon) I. Balding, Kingsclere. 18 Rn 2m 28.30 (course record)

1973
Grand National

Red Rum and Crisp

My first Grand National for the BBC had been down the course, or more accurately up the scaffolding tower, for the first televised National in 1960. If there has ever been a higher scaffolding at a race meeting I have certainly not seen it. The top was reached by a series of ladders roped on the side and once there, swaying in the wind, there was a bird's-eye view of my parish, the twelve fences north of the Melling Road.

This was the first year that the modifications to the Aintree fences had been effected – the take-off sides of all the fences had been made more inviting by sloping them. It improved the race, for by the first time at the Canal Turn there had been only three fallers. At that fence Fred Winter came down on Dandy Scot, and he climbed the tower to watch the rest of the race with me.

The following year, when Raymond Glendenning had retired from commentating, I moved to the Grandstand where I have been for the last twenty-seven Grand Nationals. I do regret swopping the country for the County Stand, for so much of the action takes place out there as Michael O'Hehir found in Foinavon's year (1967), when at the twenty-third fence there was a huge pile-up. 'There is mayhem here', is how he described this now historic event.

But even from the Grandstand the long 494-yard run-in has given me some tense and dramatic moments to describe. Ayala caught and passed Carrickbeg, ridden by John Lawrence (Lord Oaksey), in the last few agonising strides. Team Spirit and William Robinson passed four horses from the last fence to win in 1964, and then the

American chaser Jay Trump had his epic duel with Freddie to win in 1965. I suspect, though, that no one who witnessed the finish in 1973 when Red Rum caught and beat the Australian chaser Crisp will ever forget it.

The massively built Crisp, bred by his owner Sir Chester Manifold, was sent to Britain to be trained by Fred Winter for an assault on the big races at Cheltenham and Aintree. Following a long and arduous journey, Crisp won first time on a British racecourse at Wincanton on 11 March 1971 over two miles; he jumped brilliantly and won by fifteen lengths. Just five days later, and ridden by Paul Kelleway as stable jockey Richard Pitman was injured, Crisp won the Two Mile Champion Chase at the National Hunt Festival by twenty-five lengths. It was a dream start for this imposing horse who had won the hearts of everyone in the stable.

The following season Crisp's targets were to be the Gold Cup and, more ambitiously, the Grand National. In 1971–2, after two wins at three miles, he finished fourth in the Gold Cup to Glencaraig Lady. In 1973 he again ran in the National Hunt Champion Two Mile Chase and finished third to the American chaser Inkslinger.

Crisp's first appearance at Aintree created enormous interest. Although his best distance had turned out to be two and a half miles, he had jumped park fences effortlessly and he had the size of an Aintree horse – but would he stay four and a half miles? Richard Pitman had discussed tactics for the National with Fred Winter and they had both agreed that if Crisp was restrained there was the danger of him landing out on a horse ahead of him, so bold was his fencing. On the day, Crisp and Red Rum were the joint favourites at 9 to 1 as the field of thirty-eight faced the tapes.

Off they went, with Crisp and Richard Pitman on the inside, disputing the lead with Grey Sombrero on the long run to the first fence. At this point Crisp was going at a lovely swinging pace but Richard Pitman told me:

The moment he saw a fence he quickened away from the others and simply flew the fence. When we landed I just managed to take another pull to get him settled, but when he caught sight of the next, away we went again. Once we cleared the third fence, the first big ditch, I knew I was in for the ride of my life and I felt a surge of confidence which clearly went to the horse – we both kept getting braver and braver.

At Bechers Brook the drop on the inside is steeper than on the outside, but Crisp landed so far out that he met level ground, and here he took the lead. At the Canal Turn, now a long way out in front, Richard had the luxury of the course to himself and he used it to jump across to the left to make the turn easier. Crisp was so close to the inside that Richard's boot brushed the left-hand wings.

By now we in the Grandstand were getting the message from the three commentators out on the course, Michael Seth-Smith, Michael O'Hehir and Derek Thompson, that something pretty spectacular was happening, and when the field re-crossed the Melling Road back on to the racecourse, Crisp was on his own. It was an astonishing sight, and when his nearest pursuer Grey Sombrero fell at the Chair fence, Crisp went to the water jump at least twenty-five lengths in front. He took off a stride and a half too soon, but cleared it with feet to spare and then, railing round the turn, he set off on the second circuit with what appeared to be an unassailable lead.

As Crisp crossed the Melling Road Michael Seth-Smith took up the commentary. 'I have never seen in all my Nationals a horse so far ahead. He [Crisp] is over twenty lengths ahead.'

At Bechers Brook for the second time Michael O'Hehir reported: 'Crisp is almost a fence in front; he is skipping over these fences as if they were hurdles. He is twenty-five lengths in front of Red Rum in hot pursuit.'

Derek Thompson by the twenty-sixth fence gave the gap as twenty lengths, but just before he handed over to me he said: 'Crisp is twenty lengths in front but Red Rum is reducing the lead to fifteen lengths.' This suggested that Brian Fletcher on Red Rum was not prepared to settle for second place but was counting on Crisp tiring after setting such a pace.

So Crisp appeared into view of the Grandstand across

the Melling Road with just two fences to jump and then the long run-in. With a fifteen-length lead Richard Pitman was thinking of only one thing – just keeping Crisp on his feet over the last two. But running towards the last fence Richard suddenly felt Crisp falter. 'One moment he was striding forward and then his legs were going out sideways.'

Crisp struggled over the last fence, but my next statement that 'here was about to be a famous victory' now seems unfortunately premature, for as the words dried on my lips, a catastrophe seemed imminent. Horror of horrors – Crisp was now so tired that he was hardly able to raise a gallop. He had completely lost his action and Richard Pitman, using his whip in his right hand, was forcing him in towards the dolls which blank off the Chair fence. Richard Pitman is big enough to admit that he made a basic riding error by persisting with his whip in the right hand. Just in time he pulled Crisp to the right and negotiated the elbow. Now Crisp had just 220 yards to go, but to Richard this seemed the longest furlong in the world. 'The winning post never seemed to get any nearer, and then I heard Red Rum coming.'

I suspect those sounds will haunt Richard Pitman for ever, though I am sure that everyone was willing Crisp on at this stage and probably in a normal year the lead he had at the elbow would have been sufficient. But this was not a normal year, for bearing down on the almost pedestrian Crisp was Red Rum, the greatest horse of Aintree, finishing like a lion.

This is how I described the finish on *Sport on Two.*

. . . As they come to the elbow now, Crisp is under pressure – he doesn't know where he's going – Richard Pitman is trying to keep him going. Red Rum is closing the gap – defeat is facing him as Crisp has 200 yards to run and the National isn't over yet.

Crisp is keeping going – it's going to be a desperately near thing, but Crisp is walking – 25 yards to go – Red Rum goes sailing past to snatch the National. Crisp is second and the rest don't matter, for we will never see another race like that in a hundred years.

Red Rum beat Crisp by three-quarters of a length and broke the course record by nearly nineteen seconds. Crisp, whose courageous attempt to lead at such a pace had helped to set up that record, was also well inside the previous best time set up by the great Golden Miller in 1934. (Although the record for the Grand National – 9 minutes 20.4 seconds – is credited to Golden Miller, who carried 12.2, some sources quote the time of the 1935 winner Reynoldstown (11.4) as 9 minutes 20.2 seconds. Red Rum's time was 9 minutes 1.9 seconds, a speed of 29 miles per hour.)

Richard Pitman received widespread sympathy, and some criticism over the way he had ridden Crisp on the run-in. It was also a setback for Fred Winter, who had lost the Gold Cup with Pendil by a short head and had now seen another big race slip away. In spite of this, however, Fred Winter was still the leading trainer for the season. Richard said that after the race he first felt devastation but that this was swiftly followed by elation. After all, he said with certainty, 'No one ever had such a ride round Aintree.'

So Red Rum began his Grand National career, which was to set new records and which will be written about in a later chapter. But in view of his heroic race round the National course, perhaps I may be forgiven if I call the 1973 race 'Crisp's Grand National'.

LIVERPOOL, Sat., Mar. 31st 1973 (**Firm**)
GRAND NATIONAL H'CAP CHASE £25,486 £7,738: £3,794: £1,822)
4m 856yds 3.15

RED RUM 8–10–5	BFletcher	–1
Crisp (AUS) 10–12–0	RPitman	¾.2
L'Escargot 10–12–0	TCarberry	25.3
Spanish Steps 10–11–13	PBlacker	12.4
Rough Autumn 9–10–0	KWhite	2½.5
Hurricane Rock 9–10–0	RChampion	6.6
Proud Tarquin 10–10–11	LordOaksey	7
Prophecy 10–10–3	BRDavies	8

Endless Folly 11–10–0	JGuest	9
Black Secret 9–11–2	SBarker	10

S.P.: 9/1 RED RUM, Crisp, 11/1 L'Escargot, 14/1 Ashville, 16/1 Princess Camilla, Spanish Steps, Canharis, 20/1 Prophecy, Highland Seal, 22/1 Proud Tarquin, Black Secret, 25/1 Sunny Lad, Grey Sombrero. (N. le Mare) D. McCain, Birkdale, Southport, Lancs. 38 Rn 9m 1.90

1973
Finch Decanter Stakes

Wrens Hill

In a career embracing the live broadcasting of some 5000 races it is hardly surprising that some broadcasts went wrong. There have been days over the last twenty-five years when a particular race was truly memorable to me for the quite horrible moments it caused me. It is these broadcasting nightmares, the egg-on-the-face occasions, that people just love to hear about.

The Finch Decanter Stakes, run at Ascot one gloomy day in June 1973, was one example. The light was poor, and while that does not seem to matter for National Hunt racing it is more difficult on the flat, because the horses are so much more closely grouped. This was the Ascot Heath Saturday after the Royal Meeting, which always seems to me to be such an anti-climax following on from four hectic and absorbing days. There were twelve runners and the race was to be run over five furlongs. In the preview programme I had tipped Restive running in Mr R. N. Richmond-Watson's bottle-green colours. Starch Reduced, a winner the last time out with Lester Piggott riding, took the field along at full stretch with Zerbinetta and the horse I mistakenly called Restive close up. To my unbridled joy 'Restive' went to the front and I was just congratulating myself on tipping a 16 to 1 winner when, to my horror and consternation, I saw the real Restive lurking behind the leaders among the also-rans.

This is the worst moment that any commentator can go through. It's the pain barrier and a shock to the system – stark panic now sets in, the heart, I am sure, misses several beats and the mind goes numb. For while I had now correctly identified Restive, what the hell was the name of

Above left Lester Piggott in action over the sticks. Despite hitting the last flight low down, Prince Charlemagne and a youthful Lester land an enormous gamble in the 1954 Triumph Hurdle at Hurst Park – the author's first test commentary. *Right* Lester Piggott (right) on Commanche Run breaks Frank Buckle's Classic record in the 1984 Holsten Pils St Leger. Steve Cauthen (centre) on Baynoun has exerted maximum pressure, but this was Lester's day

The author pays his respects to Arkle at Tom Dreaper's stables. Mrs Betty Dreaper (now Lady Thompson) is administering sugar. Arkle was extremely sociable with his visitors

Two tough transatlantic challengers – Jay Trump and Mr Tommy Smith – foil the attempt by Freddie and Pat McCarron to be the first Scottish-trained winners of the Grand National in 1965

Sea Bird wins the 1965 Derby at a common canter, moving with a silk-like grace. The runner-up, Meadow Court, went on to win the Irish Sweeps Derby and the King George VI and Queen Elizabeth Stakes. The third, I Say (in the Reference Point colours), won the Coronation Cup as a four-year-old

Above left The author interviews Red Rum's jockey, Brian Fletcher, for *Sport on Two* in the ramshackle old BBC Radio Control Point at Aintree after Red Rum had beaten Crisp in 1973. *Right* 'You'll need a telescope to see the rest'. Shergar wins the 1981 Derby by ten lengths

Tommy Stack celebrates Red Rum's record third win in the Grand National, Red Rum looking ahead at the narrowing gap as the crowds begin to converge

The 1979 Waterford Crystal Champion Hurdle: spot the winner! Monksfield (Dessie Hughes, left) has made all the running on heavy ground and the horse appears to be tiring. Sea Pigeon has been produced by Jonjo O'Neill to challenge and looks the fresher of the two. It was Monksfield's courage that won this particular duel

The same race two years later: Daring Run (halved colours) and Mr Ted Walsh touch down with the blinkered Pollardstown (crossbelts) and Philip Blacker at the last flight. Meanwhile John Francome on Sea Pigeon (left) is perfectly poised to challenge. 'I just let the other two get on with it and I came and "did 'em" on the run-in'

this horse that had suddenly burst clear and was winning the Finch Decanter Stakes turning handsprings? In the nick of time I called it Wrens Hill, and was intensely relieved to see that its number confirmed that. As for poor old Restive, he finished a well-beaten fifth.

When such a ghastly thing happens, after the commentary one feels like digging a hole and lying in it. The colours green and dark blue, even on a murky day, do not look particularly similar when viewed close up, and I was acutely embarrassed at having to admit to misleading the listeners. I still keep the racecard in my study to remind me of what was undoubtedly the worst commentary I have ever put over. I have often tried to analyse just what went wrong over this lapse and, apart from the bad light, I think that after Royal Ascot, a twelve-runner sponsored sprint handicap simply did not get the adrenalin going fast enough. I was just exhausted after the Royal four days.

ASCOT, Sat., Jun. 23rd 1973 (Good)
FINCH DECANTER HANDICAP £4,298.30 5f

WREN'S HILL 8–3	BTaylor	–1
Super Track 7–11	DCheng	1½.2
Zerbinetta 7–9	TMcKeown	hd.3
Starch Reduced 8–8	LPiggott	5.4
Restive 7–11	PWaldron	1.5
Miss Melody 8–9	BRaymond	1.6

S.P.: 3/1 WREN'S HILL, 4/1 Starch Reduced, 6/1 Miss Melody, 9/1 Zerbinetta, 16/1 Restive, 25/1 Super Track. J. Winter, Newmarket. 12 Rn 63.4 sec

---

1974
One Thousand Guineas

Highclere

When a Classic winner in the Royal colours flashes past the post it is always a delightful event for most racegoers, and also for me as commentator. I have described Highclere winning the One Thousand Guineas and Dunfermline the St Leger. I was also present at Chantilly when Highclere won the Prix de Diane (French Oaks), but we were not broadcasting the race and I was there as a reporter.

For the 1974 One Thousand Guineas the Royal standard was fluttering over the Grandstand, indicating that Her Majesty the Queen was present to see her filly Highclere take part. The betting public rated Highclere's chances at only 12 to 1, and on her two-year-old running that was probably a fair representation. However, Major Dick Hern had produced Queen's Hussar's most famous son, Brigadier Gerard, to win the Two Thousand Guineas without a previous run, and he brought Highclere to Newmarket without her having had a race for almost seven months. In the paddock the Royal filly looked fit and well in her coat, but many were surprised to see that she was blinkered for the first time.

Mr Louis Freedman's filly Polygamy was the 4 to 1 favourite, but she seemed outpaced in the early stages; under pressure she began to improve, with half a mile to run. Meanwhile Joe Mercer had Highclere well placed, just behind the leaders and going smoothly. At the Bushes Mrs Tiggywinkle suddenly shot into the lead and looked as if she would win, but in the dip her stamina ran out and she lost her momentum and swerved to the left, just when Pat Eddery was trying to bring Polygamy through to challenge. They bumped, and this did not help Polygamy's cause, for by now Highclere was in front and running on. Polygamy staged a final effort and she ranged alongside Highclere. It was a desperate affair, both jockeys riding their hardest, and the two heads seemed absolutely in line as they crossed the finish.

I was sure that Highclere had won, but there was a nail-biting wait for the result of the photograph to be announced. Meanwhile, a huge crowd had raced round the back of the stands to be near the winners' enclosure. When Highclere was given as the winner, both Joe Mercer and Dick Hern gave a smile of sheer joy – another piece of superb training following on from Brigadier Gerard. Her Majesty looked radiant and very happy and relaxed as she greeted the first Classic winner that she had bred herself.

1974 Prix de Diane

At Chantilly, Highclere's next engagement, it was the Prix de Diane that provided us with more high drama and excitement. This race, rather than the Oaks, was chosen for Highclere as the distance, one mile two and a half furlongs, was judged more suitable. The temperature was in the nineties – it was quite the hottest day's racing I can remember. While everyone else was wilting, the Queen, who arrived on the course in a black Citroen with a motorcycle escort, looked cool and elegant in a gorgeous dress and drew gasps of admiration from the French race-goers, who pressed from all sides as she walked through the crowd to the Presidential Box.

I wondered if the heat would affect Highclere, but I need not have worried. Joe Mercer rode a patent 'safety' race, taking no chances and extremely confident that Highclere would stay. They raced in fourth place until the final turn and then Joe slipped through on the inside and took up the running nearly three furlongs out. Highclere, ridden out to the end, won emphatically by two lengths. There is no finer sight than the stylish Joe Mercer riding out a finish, and to see him in the Royal colours with Highclere moving like a dream to the winning post was one of the great moments of my racing life. On this day horse and rider made a perfect pair of ambassadors for Great Britain, while the gracious poise of the Queen won the hearts of the French racegoers.

Highclere was the first filly to take this race after winning the One Thousand Guineas, and it was also the first time that a French Classic had been won by a British Monarch. Chantilly was *en fête*, the tiny unsaddling enclosure was full of people and somewhere in the middle were Highclere and the Queen. It was some time before a path could be made, but Her Majesty seemed quite delighted at the reception that she received. It was altogether a quite remarkable atmosphere.

Joe Mercer told me that on that day he thought Highclere was a very good filly indeed.

> She seemed to sense the presence of the Queen and that this was a very special occasion. She did everything perfectly. I sent her on about three furlongs out and her response was tremendous, the French fillies just never got near her. I was worried after the race that she might react to the way the crowd were pressing round, everyone wanted to pat her, but she was as good as gold and it was a day that I shall never forget.

Nor, I suspect, will Sheilah and Dick Hern, for on the way home in their private plane a message came through from the air traffic controller that they were to be diverted to London Airport. When they landed a car was waiting which took Dick, Sheilah and Joe Mercer straight to Windsor Castle, where they had a celebration dinner as guests of the Queen.

After the race my biggest problem was to find a telephone in order to get this wonderful story on the air. There was certainly none free in the Press Room, as journalists converged on their pre-booked cubicles. I abandoned any hope of telephoning from Chantilly and set out hot-foot back to Charles de Gaulle Airport. There I was lucky to find a very helpful Air France manager who put his telephone at my disposal, and I just made the six o'clock news.

It seemed as appropriate a moment as any I can remember for us to open a bottle of Lanson in the manager's office to celebrate this particularly happy occasion.

NEWMARKET, Thur., May 2nd 1974
1,000 GUINEAS STAKES (Gr 1) £35,494.25 (£10,455: £5,127.50: £1,398.25) 1m 3.35

HIGHCLERE 9–0	JMercer	–1
Polygamy 9–0	PEddery	s.hd.2
Mrs Tiggywinkle 9–0	JGorton	4.3
Always Faithful 9–0	MKettle	3.4
Celestial Dawn 9–0	BTaylor	2.5
Lady Tan 9–0	JLindley	½.6
Red Berry 9–0	GStarkey	s.hd.7
Helmsdale 9–0	LPiggott	1½.8
Sunblast 9–0	TMcKeown	9
Bitty Girl	BRaymond	10

S.P: 4/1 Polygamy, 13/2 Mil's Bomb, 8/1 Helmsdale, 10/1 Cake, Gentle Thoughts, 11/1 Mrs Tiggywinkle, 12/1 HIGHCLERE, 14/1 Northern Gem, 16/1 Bitty Girl. (The Queen) W. Hern, West Ilsley. 1m 40.32

CHANTILLY, Sun., Jun. 16th 1974 (Good)
PRIX DE DIANE £93,549.95 1m 2f 110yds

HIGHCLERE 9–2	JMercer	–1
Comtesse de Loir	J-C Desaint	2.2
Odisea 9–2	MPhilipperon	½.3
Capaddia 9–2	GRivases	½.4
Hippodamia 9–2	WPyers	2.5
Sanperma 9–2	SLeonardos	2.6
Gaily (USA) 9–2	GLewis	½.7
Pale Ale 9–2	ELellouche	s.hd.8
Tropical Cream (USA) 9–2	JLefevre	½.9
Alumina (USA)	PEddery	1.10

S.P.: 9/2 Comtesse de Loir, 47/10 Highclere, 29/1 Odisea. (The Queen) W. Hern, West Ilsley. 22 Rn 2m 7.70

1975
King George VI and Queen Elizabeth Diamond Stakes

Grundy and Bustino

Ask any regular racegoer which was their most memorable race and they will almost surely nominate the King George VI and Queen Elizabeth Diamond Stakes run in 1975. Christopher Hawkins wrote a book about the race called *The Race of the Century*. The 1936 Gold Cup finish between Omaha and Quashed was deemed at the time to be too exciting for women to witness. In *Men and Horses I Have Known*, The Hon. George Lambton stated that he thought that the best thing in racing was when two good horses singled themselves out from the rest of the field and had a long drawn out struggle. The writer nominated the Eclipse Stakes at Sandown run in 1903, when Ard Patrick and Sceptre were involved in a long battle up the Sandown hill. Ard Patrick won that epic contest by a neck and after the race Sceptre, the beaten mare, finished the more distressed of the two.

Grundy racing against Bustino on that hot summer's day at Ascot drained the emotions, reduced strong men to tears and, in one gruelling dog fight, the future racing careers of both brave horses were extinguished.

Grundy was bought cheaply as a yearling by Keith Freeman on behalf of the Italian owner, Doctor Carlo Vittadini, and was trained at Seven Barrows by Peter Walwyn. The neat, light coloured chestnut with the flaxen mane and tail had been an outstanding two-year-old. He looked to have a favourite's chance in the Two Thousand Guineas, but a month before the race he was kicked in the face by a stable-mate while out at exercise.

It was a savage blow and at the time it seemed that the colt's chance of Classic glory had vanished. Though he was beaten in his preparatory race, the Greenham Stakes, Grundy got to the post for the Two Thousand Guineas. This proved an unsatisfactory race, for the start was delayed by striking stable lads who lined the exit to the course and prevented the runners leaving the parade ring. The race eventually started but Grundy, possibly not at his best after his setback, was beaten by the ex-Italian colt Bolkonski.

With more time available Peter Walwyn sent Grundy to the Curragh for the Irish Two Thousand Guineas, which he won very easily. We will never know whether the training setback cost Grundy that first Classic, but by Derby Day he was in tremendous form. The French-trained Green Dancer, who had won the *Observer* Gold Cup, was a serious challenger and started the 6 to 4 favourite, but at Epsom ran below his best and could only finish sixth. Grundy was invincible and stormed home from the French-trained Nobiliary by three lengths.

Meanwhile under Dick Hern's care Lady Beaverbrook's four-year-old Bustino, who had won the 1974 St Leger after finishing fourth in the Derby to Snow Knight, was building up a solid reputation at a mile and a half. He won the Coronation Cup, his only race before the King George VI and Queen Elizabeth Diamond Stakes. He was assisted in his Epsom victory by the good work done by Riboson who acted as his pacemaker. Though Bustino beat the French-trained Ashmore, he had needed all the strong driving that his capable jockey Joe Mercer could exert, after taking the lead fully two furlongs out. Dick Hern was attempting to win the top mile-and-a-half races with a horse that ideally would have been suited by racing at least two furlongs further. Riboson had made the running for Bustino in the St Leger, so it was a tragedy for the team when he went lame between Epsom and Ascot.

It is always a problem mapping out a four-year-old programme for a St Leger winner, with the preponderance of European prestige races limited to a narrow distance band between one mile and one-and-a-half miles. It is significant that only two St Leger winners have gone on to win the King George VI and Queen Elizabeth Stakes as four-year-olds; they were Ballymoss and Alcide, who achieved these Ascot victories in successive years – 1958 and 1959.

St Leger winners that attempted the double and failed include Moon Madness, Sun Princess, Dunfermline, Bruni, Sodium, Indiana, and St Paddy. However, it is worth noting that Commanche Run enjoyed tremendous success in the mile-and-a-quarter races as a four-year-old, after giving Lester Piggott his record of Classic wins in the St Leger.

With Bustino's faithful pacemaker now out of action, Dick Hern devised a plan that was used so successfully for Alycidon's assault on the 1949 Gold Cup. Like Walter Earl in 1949, he would use two pacemakers. Benny Lynch, ridden by Tommy Lowrey, and Stockbridge, by Percy Evans, were the relay team whose tactics were to burst the stamina of the American-bred Black Tarquin. How they achieved just that and how Alycidon's exceptional stamina won the day for Britain has now passed into racing legend.

I once asked a leading trainer why, when he put in a pacemaker, he always used a top-class jockey to ride it. The trainer, with a whimsical smile, said, 'You need the very best jockey available, for he has to judge the pace to a nicety, then he has to pull off the rails and allow the number one horse through.' He then added as an afterthought, 'He also has to make sure that he interferes with "the danger" as he drops back!'

As Dick Hern planned the tactics for Bustino I am sure that the last thought was furthest from his mind! He did, however, have a tremendous problem in Grundy's brilliant finishing speed. Dick's trailblazers were to be the miler Highest and the staying handicapper, Kinglet. Highest would lead from the flag, all plans depending on the horse being capable of getting to the front in a fast-run race, then Kinglet would carry the baton at least to the entrance of the straight. Then the number one horse Bustino would take over and make the best of his way home, with Grundy forced to go the pace, having the finishing burst run out of him.

It was an exciting prospect to describe a race in which the tactics were largely known in advance. The fine weather meant extremely fast ground, and an enormous crowd simply revelled in the build-up to what we all thought, quite rightly as it turned out, to be the race of the season, if not the decade. I felt some sympathy for Grundy and Pat Eddery, as it seemed to be three against one. Peter Walwyn remained confident for he knew that Grundy had come back from the Irish Derby in marvellous shape and was still improving.

The Race

Frankie Durr was the jockey entrusted to make the early running on Highest. Racing down to Swinley Bottom, they were going flat out at the head of the field who were strung out in Indian file, with Bustino fourth, followed by Grundy and Dahlia. Highest lasted until they swung right-handed at the intersection of the old mile, and then Eric Eldin on Kinglet went past the tiring miler, who dropped out as if shot. Kinglet maintained the gallop until four furlongs from home, before the entrance to the straight, where he drifted away from the rails, and Joe Mercer suddenly quickened the pace and Bustino sliced through to take up the running.

Meanwhile Pat Eddery on Grundy was enduring nightmares. The colt had never been taken along so fast in a twelve-furlong race but, with his rhythmical action, he was still hanging in. Pat was unable to influence the pace of the race, as he had to play the game according to Dick Hern's rules, but when Bustino took the lead half-a-mile out, Pat shifted Grundy into top gear and went in pursuit.

When he saw Bustino bolt round the final turn with a three-length lead, it seemed an impossible task to catch him, let alone beat him. Pat never gave up hope, and as Bustino powered away in front of him Grundy was responding. Gradually they closed on Bustino and now the lead was whittled down to two lengths and then one. With one furlong to run the two horses were level, nostrils flaring, breath pounding and both jockeys riding with a rhythm and purpose that was awesome.

Bustino, the stayer, ran the race the only way he could – out in front – and his raking stride took him closer to that small white stick with the red circle above, two hundred and twenty yards away. Grundy produced a yard of speed that carried him past Bustino by a neck, but that was immediately countered as Bustino came back at him. There is no more moving sight for me than a horse who appears to be beaten but refuses to surrender, and as the post came up Bustino, straining every sinew, knew what he had to do. This was the moment of truth, as both horses were tiring visibly. Bustino now faltered and rolled towards the rails, the race lost, and Grundy kept that half-a-length advantage on the line.

What a race for Michael Phillips of *The Times* and I to have to sum up! We were both very conscious that we had witnessed something extra special, and Michael was quick to praise the way that both the first and second horses had been prepared for this supreme contest by their trainers, Peter Walwyn and Dick Hern.

When the horses pulled up Grundy took a long time to recover and stood head down, riveted to the spot and unable to move. The race took its toll on both colts. Grundy ran once more in the Benson and Hedges Gold Cup at York where he could finish only fourth to Dahlia, whom he had beaten by five-and-a-half lengths at Ascot. He was retired after York and went to stand at the National Stud. Bustino never ran again and was retired to the Wolferton Stud, where he has been an influence for stamina. He sired the 1987 Gold Cup winner, Paean.

Grundy broke the course record for one-and-a-half miles, running it in 2 minutes 26.98 seconds. This record was later lowered on firm ground by the mare Stanerra in the 1983 Hardwick Stakes at the Royal Meeting. She set a time of 2 minutes 26.95 seconds, which surprised me for I never thought that Grundy's time would be beaten.

Both horses put up as game a performance as I have ever witnessed, and the race recalled those legendary tales of the matches between The Flying Dutchman and Great Voltigeur at York, Ard Patrick and Sceptre at Sandown, and Omaha and Quashed at Ascot. There was no television action replay in those days, but present-day racegoers may have to wait some time before they see another race to compare with Grundy beating Bustino in the sun at Ascot. I consider myself lucky to have been there to describe it.

ASCOT, Sat., July 26th 1975 (Firm)
KING GEORGE VI AND QUEEN ELIZABETH DIAMOND STAKES £81,910 1½m

GRUNDY 3–8–7	PEddery	–1
Bustino 4–9–7	JMercer	½.2
Dahlia (USA) 5–9–4	LPiggott	5.3
On My Way (USA) 5–9–7	WPyers	1½.4
Card King (USA) 7–9–7	RJallu	½.5
Ashmore (FR) 4–9–7	YSaint-Martin	1½.6

S.P.: 4/5 Grundy, 4/1 Bustino, 6/1 Dahlia, 13/1 Star Appeal.
(Dr C. Vittadini) P. Walwyn, Lambourn. 11 Rn 2m 26.98

1975
St Leger

Bruni

Bruni's ten-length win in the 1975 St Leger was an achievement that meant everything to Ryan Price, who trained him, and to Tony Murray, who rode him with such skill and artistry. Ryan had bought Bruni cheaply as a yearling for only 7800 guineas, and his absolute faith in the horse was totally vindicated on Town Moor. Ryan had trained the dam Bombazine to win three times as a two-year-old and to finish fourth in the Oaks and the Ribblesdale Stakes at Royal Ascot. Bruni turned out to be the mare's first winner.

Charles St George owned Bruni, but Ryan had been able to run the colt only once as a two-year-old. He had proved far too impetuous on the gallops and with a staying pedigree he had to be taught to settle. Bruni proved to be a real character – he wanted things all his own way. Con Horgan, Ryan Price's assistant, said that no gallop with Bruni in it ever went according to plan; Bruni saw to that. He refused to wait his turn, cavorting and plunging, and he became very skilful at 'dropping' his rider. The riderless Bruni racing across the Downs on his own was a fairly common sight. Ryan would send him for long hacks across the downs, far from the rest of the string, and this patient handling worked, for he made up into a strong and athletic three-year-old, much of the credit for which goes to one of Ryan's best work riders, 'Jerry' German, Bruni's regular partner on these 'country walks'.

Tony Murray rode Bruni in his early races and, after running second in the Tudor Stakes at Sandown after a slow start, he won over a mile and a quarter at Salisbury. In the Predominate Stakes at Goodwood he finished a short head second to No Alimony and on the strength of that run the owner wanted Lester Piggott, then without a Derby ride, to partner the colt at Epsom.

Against Ryan's advice, Bruni ran in the Derby with Lester Piggott in the saddle. The horse was far too inexperienced for a race like the Derby and had a rough passage, carried wide at Tattenham Corner. He finished very sore, and promptly caught a virus, as did so many of the inmates of Soldiers Field that summer. But by August Bruni had recovered, and Ryan began to prepare him for the St Leger, running him in a ten-furlong conditions race at the Variety Club meeting at Sandown. Even though he had not run since the Derby, Bruni started at odds on and won easily, breaking the course record. Ryan was elated and told the owner that he would win the St Leger, though he was greeted with disbelief for the bush telegraph from Ballydoyle was sounding King Pellinore, who was to be ridden by Charles St George's friend Lester Piggott.

On the opening day of the St Leger meeting Ryan Price saddled Treasury Bond to win the Rous Nursery Stakes under top weight, after a three-month lay-off. The horses were now running well and Ryan's confidence was further increased when Royal Match, whom Bruni had beaten at Sandown, won the Town Moor Handicap on the Thursday. Ryan was very bullish – the distance was right, the horse was in prime condition and he feared nothing. I have never known the trainer to be so confident.

King Pellinore, second to Grundy in the Irish Sweeps Derby, was the favourite, and he and Consol, who had just won the Geoffrey Freer Stakes at Newbury, were the main opponents for Bruni, who went off at 9 to 1 having touched 15 to 2 and 7 to 1.

Tony Murray settled Bruni without difficulty. Consol made the running at a fast pace, but Murray sat still as a mouse. The grey felt powerful under him and he realised quite early in the straight that he had every other runner beaten. In my commentary I remarked just how easily Bruni appeared to be travelling, and then Tony gave him just a few more inches of rein and the colt strode majestically to the front and quickly opened up a lead of ten lengths over King Pellinore, who was left labouring in his wake. Ten lengths was the winning distance. Only Never Say Die won the final Classic by a wider margin, and Provoke and Talma II also won by ten lengths.

Tony Murray took no end of pleasure in putting one over Lester Piggott, though it was Lester who took over the ride on Bruni the following year when Tony Murray left Findon in order to ride in France. Although Lester won the Yorkshire Cup and the Cumberland Lodge, he finished second in both the Hardwick at Royal Ascot and in the King George VI and Queen Elizabeth Diamond Stakes. In each of these costly Ascot defeats Bruni had swerved at the start and lost ground. In the King George, Lester had lost a stirrup iron and Ryan Price was not impressed with his riding and said so in the hearing of the racing press. The fact was that Lester never really got on with Bruni – he restrained him with a grip like a half-nelson, and the colt used to fight him. Murray's more sympathetic and gentler approach was more effective.

Bruni was Ryan Price's second Classic winner – his first had been the filly Ginevra (also owned by Charles St George) who had won the Oaks ridden by Tony Murray in 1972.

DONCASTER, Sat., Sept. 13th 1975 (Good)
ST LEGER STAKES (Gr 1) £52,131.35 (£15,281: £7,440.50: £1,952.15) 1m 6f 127yds 3.00

BRUNI 9–0	AMurray	–1
King Pellinore (USA) 9–0	LPiggott	10.2
Libra's Rib (USA) 9–0	WCarson	1½.3
Hobnob (FR) 9–0	BRaymond	nk.4
Consol 9–0	PEddery	5.5
Miss Toshiba (USA) 8–11	ABond	1.6
Stamen (USA) 9–0	GBaxter	7
Whip it Quick 9–0	PWaldron	8

S.P.: 2/1 King Pellinore, 9/2 Consol, 11/2 Sea Anchor, 9/1 BRUNI, 13/1 Hunza Dancer, 15/1 Stamen. (C. A. B. St George) Ryan Price, Findon. 12 Rn 3m 5.31

1977
News of the World Grand National

Red Rum

It has been said that it was fortunate that Arkle had Tom Dreaper as a trainer. That wise old man knew what he had and brought that great chaser to his full potential slowly and patiently. A similar story applies to Red Rum, for I doubt if this remarkable Aintree horse would have reached the heights he did had he not been trained on Southport Sands by Donald ('Ginger') McCain.

What I find so extraordinary about Red Rum's life story, so vividly portrayed in Ivor Herbert's book *Red Rum*, is that two well-known supporters of National Hunt racing, Mr Maurice Kingsley and Mrs Lurlene Brotherton, somehow allowed this horse to slip through their hands. Four trainers – Tim Molony, Bobbie Renton, Tommy Stack (for three months) and Tony Gillam – had care of Red Rum before he was weeded out and sold by Mrs Brotherton just seven months before his first Grand National win.

By the time Ginger McCain bought him for 6000 guineas at Doncaster August Sales in 1972 he had already had one life and now, in the unconventional surroundings of a stable behind a second-hand car lot in Birkdale, Lancashire, with the fifth trainer of his career, he started another.

Clearly the gelding thrived on the unconventional routine and his work on the sands, for on 30 September, ridden by Tommy Stack, he won first time out at Carlisle for the new stable. This was followed by four more wins at Wetherby, Newcastle, Haydock and at Ayr, where Brian Fletcher began his association with the horse. From relative obscurity Ginger McCain had proved with his handling of Red Rum and another 'cast-off', Glenkiln, that his unorthodox method of training did actually work. The racing press now began to take notice of the remarkable success story of Ginger and Beryl McCain.

The plan was to run Red Rum in the Grand National, and the Greenall Whitley Chase at Haydock Park was to be his preparatory race. On 3 March he finished a respectable fourth to Tregarron before his first Grand National win. Ginger subsequently used this race every year from 1973 to 1978 as Red Rum's pre-National race. In those six years Red Rum finished: fourth – unseated rider – fourth – fifth – sixth – sixth. In 1974 he was cannoned into at the second fence and Brian Fletcher was sent flying out of the saddle. Without a rider 'Rummy' continued in the race and jumped every fence, returning none the worse, and three weeks later he won his second Grand National.

For the 1974 Grand National Red Rum's weight had gone up from 10 stone 5 lb to 12 stone, a rise of 23 lb. On good ground seventeen horses finished, but nothing finished in front of Red Rum, who beat L'Escargot by seven lengths and joined the select band of seven horses who had won the race twice. (The last had been Reynoldstown in 1936.) The following month Red Rum also won the Scottish National under 11 stone 13 lb.

In 1975 Red Rum again carried 12 stone at Aintree, but was set to give the dual Gold Cup winner L'Escargot 11 lb, which meant that L'Escargot was now 10 lb better in with him for a seven-length beating the previous year. Well as Red Rum ran in the National, L'Escargot was too strong for him on the run-in and Red Rum was beaten by fifteen lengths into second place. Two wins and a second in three years had the historians searching for the record books. Cloister was the horse with which Red Rum was now being compared, for this great chaser was the only horse to have finished in the first two in three consecutive years. He had twice finished second before winning in 1893.

The following year Red Rum was dropped 2 lb in the Grand National handicap, and he carried 11 stone 10 lb. Tommy Stack rode him that year, thus renewing the partnership that had started at Ripon when, for a short time, Tommy had taken over Bobbie Renton's licence. Tommy had also been aboard for Red Rum's first win for Donald McCain. This year the concession of 12 lb to Fred Rimell's Rag Trade proved too much, and so once again Red Rum came out second best, beaten two lengths. Red Rum now created another record, for no horse had ever finished in the first two four years in succession.

By the time that the 1977 National weights were published Red Rum had won only a three-horse race at Carlisle and the general impression was that he was beginning to show his age, which is probably why the handicapper gave him his lowest National weight for four years – 11 stone 8 lb. At the age of twelve he still started 9 to 1 co-second favourite, the market leader being Andy Pandy trained, like Rag Trade, by Fred Rimell; Andy Pandy had won the Malcolm Fudge National Trial at Haydock. Also in the field were the Gold Cup winner Davy Lad, who had only 10 stone 13 lb, and the Hennessy and Mildmay winner Zeta's Son.

The Race

So Red Rum returned for the fifth time to Aintree, and on a bright sunny day he paraded with his old friend Tommy Stack in the saddle. Watching them walking around before the start I marvelled at Tommy's coolness and composure. It was a race full of incident, and on this day the luck most certainly went Tommy's way.

No fewer than seven horses fell at the first fence and Gold Cup hero Davy Lad went at the third. The field, headed by Sebastian V, thundered towards the mighty Bechers Brook where Michael O'Hehir reported the fall of the leader; already thirteen of the field were out of the race. When the runners streamed across the Melling Road back on to the racecourse, the leader by twenty lengths was the 66 to 1 outsider Boom Docker, who had his moment of glory jumping the water with a lead similar to that of Crisp four years earlier. Michael Seth-Smith took up the commentary as Boom Docker refused at the seventeenth fence; this left Andy Pandy in the lead from What A Buck, Hidden Value and Roman Bar, with Red Rum fifth.

At Bechers for the second time Michael O'Hehir had Andy Pandy ten lengths clear, and then came: 'Andy Pandy's down in the lead, so is Nereo and he's interfered with What A Buck; and now Red Rum takes the lead.' The second part of his commentary, broadcast as the National is over the public address system, was drowned by the roar of disappointment from the crowd, and the only people who could see the tremendous advantage that Red Rum now had were those actually at Bechers and the millions of radio listeners and television viewers all around the world.

We then heard Derek Thompson, his voice quivering with emotion and excitement, call Red Rum three lengths ahead of Churchtown Boy with three more fences to jump. The Grandstand crowd was now on tiptoe and the atmosphere intense. Remembering the disappointment that we had all felt when Crisp had been caught four years earlier, the last thing I wanted to do at this stage was to anticipate a win that would not happen. I was also concerned about the antics of two loose horses that had dogged Red Rum from the Canal Turn, but when Tommy Stack steered Red Rum to the left-hand rails approaching the second-last fence, they galloped on past the fence. Red Rum now had Churchtown Boy, ridden by Martin Blackshaw, as his nearest challenger. But they clouted that fence hard, which Tommy heard. So Red Rum increased his lead slightly as they came to the last fence.

I hardly dared to say anything, and waited silently for a safe jump. A fall at the last was too horrible to contemplate and so, with 65,000 others, I held my breath. The roar of relief from the crowd said everything, and Red Rum was safely over. Now for the 494-yard run-in. Again for a moment the riderless horses threatened to gallop across Red Rum, but at the last minute they veered away. I said:

Tommy Stack now sets his heart for home – behind him eight lengths away comes Churchtown Boy but he is *not* going to catch Red Rum.

Here comes the greatest horse of Aintree. Red Rum has 200 yards to run to make history.

Two riderless horses are in front – Tommy Stack is pushing Red Rum – the excitement here is tremendous.

Red Rum has done it for the *third* time – Red Rum the toast of Aintree. The public are on the course, everyone is going mad!

It was an emotional moment for Lord Oaksey and me in the commentary box, as we watched the most amazing scenes that we had ever seen on a British racecourse. It had been an incredible race. Not many recordings of my commentaries are used in 'pop' records, but this was merged into the record 'Red Rum's Song', made by Kevin Parrott who had also had the hit record 'Matchstalk Men and Matchstalk Cats and Dogs'. 'Red Rum's Song' did not reach as high in the charts, but it gets a playing each year when Grand National time comes round.

In retrospect I cannot help admiring Tommy Stack's *sang-froid* and the totally professional way he rode from the Canal Turn home. Years later I asked what was then going through his mind. He admitted that the loose horses had given him some anxiety, but he gave credit to Red Rum's intelligence and concentration. 'It is a long way from the Melling Road to the winning post when you're in front in the National.'

Tommy will never forget that lonely three-quarters of a mile. He knew that it was Martin Blackshaw and Churchtown Boy following but when Red Rum jumped the second-last fence cleanly and quickly he heard a frightful crash behind and he knew that his pursuer had hit the fence hard. He now forced himself to concentrate on keeping Red Rum balanced and on a good stride going to the last fence. Once safely over he was not going to let Red Rum relax, and kept on pushing him out with hands and heels, taking the centre of the course for safety after the elbow. Then it was all over, and he found the crowd spilling across the course. His last thought, professional to the end, was to look down to see that the weight cloth was still in place – two stone of lead lying somewhere out on the course would not have amused the Clerk of the Scales when he weighed in.

To win the race for the third time was an outstanding feat of training by Donald McCain. For each of the last five years he had delivered Red Rum to the post in peak fitness, and to be beaten by a whisker for the Hennessy Gold Cup and to win the Scottish National under 11 stone 13 lb showed that Red Rum was just as good away from Aintree.

At midnight on the evening of the Grand National, Red Rum was still on parade. The police cleared the road outside the Bold Hotel in Southport, and Red Rum made an appearance in the ballroom. The owner of the hotel, John Craig, had said to Ginger McCain that if they won the National he would host a party for Red Rum, and so he kept to his bargain. They had to remove the swing doors and they placed a carpet down, and through the bar and past the dining room walked the horse that a few hours earlier had galloped four and a half miles.

Tommy Stack was there and said that everyone wanted to pat the horse, who looked absolutely marvellous and did not turn a hair. 'He was such an intelligent horse he took everything in and enjoyed all the adulation; he seemed to realise that he had just done something rather special.'

There was at one time the prospect of Red Rum returning to try for win number four, but he developed a strain of the tendon to the pedal bone and this was one race that Ginger McCain lost, for he was withdrawn on the eve of what would have been his sixth appearance in the National. Red Rum was now retired, but made a guest appearance before the race. Tommy Stack, who had been severely injured in a fall in the paddock at Hexham, made a brave and courageous bid to get fit to ride Rummy. After intense workouts in the gymnasium Tommy returned to ride early in March, with the incentive that he would be reunited with his favourite horse. But it was not to be, and Tommy rode Hidden Value who got only as far as the second fence.

Red Rum then went into show business and travelled the country opening supermarkets, pubs and betting shops. He appeared at numerous horse shows, and I still have the script that I wrote for one of these appearances.

To look at Red Rum who would think that he had competed in a hundred National Hunt races or had started his career as a two-year-old in 1967 by winning a seller at Aintree? He holds three records: he has won three Grand Nationals; he has finished first or second in five consecutive Nationals; and he holds the course record for the Grand National. He has jumped 150 Grand National fences without falling and covered twenty-two miles at racing pace round Aintree.

He has won twenty-four of his hundred races over the jumps and three on the flat – a total of twenty-seven.

In all he raced over three hundred miles and jumped 1800 fences without ever falling – testimony of his constitution, his courage and his extreme intelligence. Not a bad buy for 400 guineas.

LIVERPOOL, Sat., Apr. 2nd 1977 (Good)
NEWS OF THE WORLD GRAND NATIONAL CHASE
(H'cap) £41,140 (£12,520: £6,160: £2,980) 4m 4f 3.15

Horse	Jockey	
RED RUM 12–11–8	TStack	–1
Churchtown Boy 10–10–0	MBlackshaw	25.2
Eyecatcher 11–10–1	CRead	6.3
The Pilgarlic 9–10–4	REvans	6.4
Forest King 8–10–12	RCrank	4.5
What a Buck 10–11–4	JKing	4.6
Happy Ranger 10–10–5	PBlacker	7
Carroll Street 10–10–0	RLinley	8
Collingwood 11–10–1	CHawkins	9
Hidden Value 9–10–4	TBourke	10
Saucy Belle 11–10–0	RFDavies	11

S.P.: 15/2 Andy Pandy, 9/1 RED RUM, Gay Vulgan, 10/1 Davy Lad, 15/1 Pengrail, 16/1 War Bonnett, Winter Rain, 18/1 Prince Rock, Zeta's Son, Eyecatcher, 20/1 What a Buck, Sir Garnet, Sage Merlin, Churchtown Boy. (N. le Mare) D. McCain, Birkdale, Southport, Lancs. 42 Rn 9m 30.30

Speed and Stamina at Royal Ascot

Between the covers of my precious Royal Ascot reference book are the results in depth of each of the twenty-four races run at the Royal meeting since 1945. Only a few of those post-war races were broadcast, and when I took over the radio commentaries in 1961 we covered only the Ascot Stakes, the Royal Hunt Cup, the Gold Cup and the Wokingham Stakes. As far as the betting public was concerned it was the big Ascot handicaps that were important.

It was not until the Duke of Norfolk's Committee Report on the Pattern of Racing that the 'conditions' races, as they were known, were identified, and following Lord Porchester's Flat Race Planning Committee's recommendations in 1967 these races were absorbed into the international Group system and given Group rankings. Of all the innovations that have been introduced into racing during my term as BBC racing correspondent, I rate the Group system, supported with finance from the Levy Board, as the most significant.

Royal Ascot is the 'shop window' for racing – a win in any of the Group races provides enormous prestige for the horse that wins it as well as for his sire and dam. There is no sponsorship, and nowhere can you see so many Group races in four days. It has been the development of the Group races that has brought popularity of an almost alarming degree to the Royal meeting. The St James's Palace Stakes was always run as the last race of the day on the Tuesday and the King's Stand Stakes, or the 'getting out stakes' as it was known, was the very last race of the meeting on the Friday. There was often an astonishing volume of betting.

On the opening day of Ascot in 1987 there were four Group 2 races and one Group 3, with the Ascot Stakes as the last race of the day.

1977 Gold Cup – *Sagaro*

The Gold Cup, run over two and a half miles, used to be considered one of the most important races in the calendar, but as the demand is for more speed, breeders give Gold Cup winners the cold shoulder. One of the most famous finishes for the Gold Cup was that fought out in 1936 by the four-year-old mare Quashed and the American horse Omaha. It was so gruelling and exciting a contest that women were reported to have fainted in the aisles. Quashed was hailed as the 'greatest mare of all time'. Of course, it was Britain versus America, and the Gold Cup is one race that American-bred horses just do not win.

Notable winners in the last few years have been Ragstone, who carried the colours of Her Majesty's Representative at Ascot, The Duke of Norfolk, and Precipice Wood, ridden so stylishly by Jimmy Lindley, who won in 1970, and was trained by Mrs Rosemary Lomax, who became the first women to train a winner at the Royal meeting.

The best Gold Cup winners since the war have been Alycidon, who had two pacemakers, and the subsequent Prix de l'Arc de Triomphe winner Levmoss. More recently, three high-class stayers in Le Moss, Ardross and Gildoran all scored double wins, and helped to raise the status of the race. Pride of place in the record book, though, must go to the French-trained Sagaro, who won a record three Gold Cups from 1975.

The Race

Sagaro had already joined the select band of horses who had won the race twice, but when he returned to Ascot to try to win for a record third time the indications were not promising. In the run-up to the race he had been defeated three times in France by Buckskin, owned by Daniel Wildenstein. In the Prix du Cadran, the French equivalent of the Gold Cup which is run in May, Sagaro came to win for the second year running, but he could not maintain his lead and Buckskin rallied and snatched the race close to home. It sounded as if jockey Philippe Pacquet came too soon on Sagaro and for Ascot, Lester Piggott was back in the saddle.

The going was yielding and Buckskin was the 2 to 1 favourite with Sagaro and the St Leger winner Bruni at 9 to 4. The French horse Citoyen, ridden by the Australian jockey Bill Pyers, made the running from Buckskin and Sagaro. Seven furlongs from home Yves St Martin took Buckskin to the front and stepped up the pace, but Sagaro moved easily into second place. Rounding the the final turn Yves St Martin tried to get away from his tail, but hard as he rode to get Buckskin out of reach, Lester just sat behind on Sagaro, still full of running. A furlong from the finish Lester simply cruised up to Buckskin and passed him in a few strides to win at a canter by five lengths. Buckskin was second and Citoyen third, an all-French finish. Bruni had swallowed his tongue and ran in at fourth place after wandering about in the last two furlongs.

This was Lester Piggott's eighth win in the race, a total he was to increase to eleven before he retired. The race could, it seemed, have been made for this tactical genius. Sagaro set a new record, for no horse had ever won three Gold Cups, and he was promptly retired. With Levy Board money Sagaro was bought by the National Stud for a figure of £175,000. Sad to say, he was not a success at stud and died in 1986.

1986 King's Stand Stakes – *Last Tycoon*

The King's Stand Stakes is one of the most thrilling races of the meeting, if not the year. A Group 1 race over five furlongs (demoted to Group 2 in 1988), it always attracts a high-class field, never more so than in 1970 when Amber Rama scorched home from a field of great sprinters to win in a course record time. The northern sprinter Chris had previously held the record from 1959, but Amber Rama, who had previously finished fourth in the Two Thousand Guineas to Nijinsky, was the first horse to break the one-minute barrier over Ascot's five furlongs. He clocked 59.27 seconds, and the list of sprinters that he beat is formidable: Huntercombe, Balidar, Prince Tenderfoot, Raffingora, Jukebox and Tribal Chief. Only two other horses have beaten sixty seconds – that superb sprinter Bay Express in 1974 and Last Tycoon in 1986.

Sadly I did not broadcast Amber Rama's win, which is probably just as well for I did take a bit of the 9 to 2 on offer and was able to give him no end of vocal assistance in the last furlong. I did, however, commentate on the outstanding race in 1986 won by Last Tycoon.

The Race

This was a tremendously interesting betting race with three horses heavily supported. Robert Sangster's five-year-old Double Schwartz opened at 3 to 1, came in to 2 to 1 and finally settled at 9 to 4 favourite. The three-year-old filly Gwydion, who opened at 9 to 4, went briefly to 7 to 2 before closing at 100 to 30, while the French-trained Last Tycoon, who had won his two previous races in France, opened at 4 to 1 and started at 9 to 2. The American jockey Cash Asmussen stood in for Yves St Martin, Last Tycoon's regular jockey, who had been injured.

There had been only two French-trained winners of the King's Stand – Amber Rama in 1970 and Flirting Around in 1975. Last Tycoon, trained by Robert Collet at Chantilly, was badly drawn at fourteen of the fourteen runners, on the extreme outside. He was ridden differently to his previous wins, when he had been covered up, and Asmussen lay handy in third place as outsiders Amigo Loco and then Stalker made the running. When they dropped out Steve Cauthen took over on Gwydion, but she was immediately challenged by Last Tycoon. Meanwhile Pat Eddery was beginning to make ground on Double Schwartz and entering the final furlong he came bursting through to challenge Last Tycoon. Such was the momentum with which Double Schwartz arrived that I thought it would carry him past the French colt. Not a bit of it. Cash Asmussen, riding his hardest, encouraged Last Tycoon to counter this challenge. Now we had a real race on our hands as they battled away with hardly an inch separating them.

It was an interesting study in riding styles between the best of two countries. Now was not the time, though, to start making comparisons and as they flashed past the post I thought I saw Last Tycoon's nose ahead and called him the winner from Double Schwartz. It was risky for in the Cork and Orrery Stakes on the previous day I had been equally convinced that Willie Carson on Cyrano de Bergerac had got up in the very last stride to shade Sperry, but I had been wrong and Sperry had won by a short head.

It was therefore with some relief that I heard the announcer call Last Tycoon the winner and Double Schwartz second, with Gwydion third. The time was the second fastest ever, 59.28 seconds, compared with Amber Rama's 59.27 seconds. That they were two very high-class sprinters I had no doubt – Last Tycoon should have won the three British Group 1 sprints, but didn't. Yves St Martin rode one of his rare bad races in the July Cup and Last Tycoon finished only fourth to Green Desert. At York Last Tycoon showed how misleading the Newmarket form had been by winning the William Hill Sprint Championship and beating Green Desert.

Last Tycoon was then prepared for the Breeders Cup Mile in which he covered himself with glory by proving the only European-trained winner in the Breeders Cup series, and the first European winner of the Mile. Double Schwartz, after being beaten in the Vernons Cup, won the Prix de l'Abbaye at Longchamp on Arc day.

On that day at Ascot it was a joy to see the speed at which they finished, and it demonstrated that there is room for horses of the highest class at both ends of the spectrum – speed and stamina.

ROYAL ASCOT, Jun. 16th 1977 (Good)
GOLD CUP (Gr 1) £17,837.50 (£5,350: £2,575: £1,187.50)
2m 4f 3.45

SAGARO 6–9–0	LPiggott	–1
Buckskin (FR) 4–9–0	YSaint-Martin	5.2
Citoyen 5–9–0	WPyers	2.3
Bruni 5–9–0	BTaylor	7.4
Bright Finish (USA) 4–9–0	PEddery	15.5
Centrocon 4–8–11	PWaldron	5.6

S.P.: 2/1 Buckskin, 9/4 SAGARO, Bruni, 10/1 Bright Finish. (G. A. Oldham) F. Boutin, France. 6 Rn 4m 29.87

ROYAL ASCOT, Fri., June 20th 1986 (Firm)
KING'S STAND STAKES (Gr 1) £48,828 5f

LAST TYCOON 3–8–9	CAsmussen	–1
Double Schwartz 5–9–3	PatEddery	s.hd.2
Gwydion 3–8–6	SCauthen	2½.3
Welsh Note 3–8–6	TIves	4.4
Polykratis 4–9–3	JReid	½.5
Sharp Romance 4–9–3	RCochrane	nk.6
Fayruz 3–8–9	PWaldron	¾.7
Storm Warning 4–9–0	WRSwinburn	½.8
Hallgate 3–8–9	WCarson	¾.9
Atall Atall 3–8–9	MKinane	nk.10

S.P.: 9/4 Double Schwartz, 100/30 Gwydion, 9/2 LAST TYCOON, 9/1 Hallgate, 12/1 Nomination, 16/1 Stalker, Welsh Note, 20/1 Atall Atall, Storm Warning. (Mr R. Strauss) R. Collet, France. 14 Rn 59.28 sec

1979 & 1981
Waterford Crystal Champion Hurdle

Monksfield and Sea Pigeon

Cheltenham is my favourite racecourse. The radio commentary position there is the best that we have and I look forward every year to the National Hunt Festival, a three-day feast of racing to thrill all jumping enthusiasts.

I have included Arkle and Dawn Run winning the Gold Cup in 1964 and 1986, but the Champion Hurdle has also provided some superb spectacles, such as the six vintage races run from 1976 to 1981, in which those three remarkable hurdlers Night Nurse, Monksfield and Sea Pigeon were dominant. It is difficult to know which year to choose, and the permutations of their placings over those six years are quite extraordinary as the table shows.

Champion Hurdle

1976	**1979**
Night Nurse	Monksfield
Bird's Nest	Sea Pigeon
Flash Imp	Beacon Light
1977	**1980**
Night Nurse	Sea Pigeon
Monksfield	Monksfield
Dramatist	Bird's Nest
Sea Pigeon	
1978	**1981**
Monksfield	Sea Pigeon
Sea Pigeon	Pollardstown
Night Nurse	Daring Run

Each of the three won two years in succession, but the races I have selected are the 1979 and 1981 Waterford Crystal Champion Hurdles. My first reference point was Jonathan Powell's immensely enjoyable book on Monksfield, and in the first chapter I found this nugget.

The sustained duel between Monksfield and Sea Pigeon in March 1979, in driving rain and deep clinging mud, was the most enthralling finish ever seen on Cheltenham Hill in the 52-year history of the Champion Hurdle. Eight other horses paraded with them beforehand, but they were relegated to the role of bit players as the two principal actors were locked together in combat over the final 3 furlongs.

Reference to the chart reveals that Monksfield and Sea Pigeon were old duellists and in 1978 Monksfield, the runner-up the previous year, had beaten Sea Pigeon by two lengths, so the score before the 1979 race was one-nil to Monksfield.

Monksfield was unusual in that he was an entire, whereas most male chasers and hurdlers are geldings, and a six-year-old horse can be a handful. Some trainers, for example Ryan Price, managed to win many races with full horses such as Nuage Dore, Eborneezer, Cantab and Sir d'Orient, and Monksfield was just his sort of horse. The 1978 win had brought a young trainer, Des McDonogh, into the spotlight and the way he produced little Monksfield to win at Cheltenham and at Aintree was in the style of Vincent O'Brien's well-planned raids of the fifties.

Monksfield hated the cold and as the winter of 1979 lingered on, his preparation races for Cheltenham did not go according to plan. Top weight in the Sweeps hurdle, he finished a creditable third. However, in the Erin Foods Champion Hurdle at Fairyhouse in February, different tactics were employed and he was held up in a slowly run race, finishing well behind, and his jockey Tommy Kinane lost the ride in the Champion Hurdle. So for the National Hunt Festival Dessie Hughes replaced Kinane while on Sea Pigeon Jonjo O'Neill took over from Frank Berry, who had ridden the horse the previous year. The going had become heavy following some appalling March weather, and Dessie Hughes took Monksfield to the front from the start and raced wide on fresh ground that had not been poached by the previous three hurdle races run over the old course (the Champion Hurdle is now run on the opening day of the meeting, thus ensuring better ground conditions for the hurdling crown), so Monksfield on the outside led all the way. Though Sea Pigeon was hating the ground he moved ominously up to Monksfield as they came down the hill, with Kybo a danger to them both. Sadly Kybo fell heavily two out and it was now a duel with no quarter given or asked between Monksfield and Sea Pigeon.

As they rounded the final turn Monksfield came wide and headed for the rails on the stands side. Dessie Hughes was hard at work but the horse was not giving away an inch, yet when Jonjo O'Neill asked Sea Pigeon to challenge, the race looked a foregone conclusion, for he seemed to be sitting on a double handful. Both horses jumped the last flight brilliantly, but Jonjo was nursing Sea Pigeon for a last final spurt. Half-way up the run-in it still seemed to be Sea Pigeon's race. Dessie never gave up and Monksfield never flinched from the whip – he just kept grinding on up the hill, head outstretched, giving his all. Then an extraordinary thing happened. From looking all over the winner, Sea Pigeon now began to flag and Jonjo went for his whip. Slowly, but with ever-increasing confidence in the brave horse under him, Dessie Hughes felt Monksfield take Sea Pigeon's measure and, with bursting lungs and pounding heart, he stretched away inch by inch from Sea Pigeon. On the line, Monksfield won by three-quarters of a length.

Seeing the race again and again on the re-run it was hard to believe at any stage that Monksfield would prove to be the winner, and I suspect that Jonjo thought that this time Sea Pigeon would gain his revenge. I shall never forget the way that Monksfield overcame the dreadful conditions on that day; he surely deserved an equine bravery award.

Monksfield retired to the Anngrove Stud at Mountmellick, Portlaoise in Ireland, and stands alongside Sexton

Blake and Pollerton. He had his first winners in 1986, one of them Black Monkey who won a 'Bumpers' and was bought to be trained by David Nicholson. On New Year's Day 1988, Monksfield had his first Cheltenham winner when David saddled Black Monkey to win Division I of the Woodcote Novice Hurdle.

Although the Hurdle Championship still eluded him, Sea Pigeon was not only a superb hurdler but also one of the best long-distance handicappers on the flat. He had won the Ladbroke Chester Cup two years running in 1978 and 1979, and had then taken the Tote Ebor Handicap at York with a record 10 stone when ridden by Jonjo O'Neill. A truly versatile gelding, he was also extremely well bred, being by Sea Bird II out of a Round Table mare called Around The Roses, but because he had proved difficult to handle he was gelded in the autumn of his three-year-old days when trained at Beckhampton by Jeremy Tree. All of this is recounted in greater detail in Bill Curling's delightful book *The Sea Pigeon Story*.

Sea Pigeon's preparation for the 1980 Champion Hurdle did not go smoothly. He bruised his near fore hoof and Peter Easterby was unable to give him a race before the Festival meeting, leaving the stable hopeful rather than confident.

It was once again heavy ground for the Festival and, incredibly, for the third year running the two horses rounding the final turn in the Champion Hurdle with one flight to jump were Monksfield and Sea Pigeon. Once over the last flight, however, the race took a different turn, for Sea Pigeon raced up the hill and left Monksfield toiling seven lengths behind. Sea Pigeon had won the Waterford Crystal Champion Hurdle at his fourth attempt. In *The Sea Pigeon Story* Bill Curling reminds us that for 1980 the Champion Hurdle course had been shortened by 200 yards by cutting out the top bend beyond the stands. This made the distance exactly two miles, and the change was very much in Sea Pigeon's favour. It was a very popular win and Sea Pigeon was voted National Hunt Racehorse of the Year.

Jonjo O'Neill had ridden Sea Pigeon both on the flat

Speed at Royal Ascot: a pulsating finish for the 1986 King's Stand Stakes. Last Tycoon (hoops, far side) shades Robert Sangster's Double Schwartz (noseband) by a short head in the second fastest time the race has ever been run. *Inset* My racecard

The 1985 General Accident One Thousand Guineas: Oh So Sharp lands the first leg of her fillies' Triple Crown, but needed every inch of the Rowley Mile to do so. A short head separates her from the second, Al Bahathri (centre, noseband) ridden by Tony Murray, and Bella Colora (white cap, far side) with Lester Piggott is another short head away in third. The fourth filly (right) is Vilikaia

Above left The 1986 Tote Cheltenham Gold Cup: Dawn Run and Jonjo O'Neill surrounded by well-wishers after winning the most astonishing race for the Gold Cup. It was like the days of Arkle at the Festival again. *Right* The Princess Royal receives the congratulations of the Queen and the Queen Mother after winning the Dresden Diamond Stakes at Ascot on 25 July 1987

The 1987 Ever Ready Derby: Reference Point makes every yard of the running to win in near record time and, following Slip Anchor, gave Steve Cauthen his second Derby in three years

'Did Sassafras win the Arc or did Nijinsky lose it?' Even allowing for the angle of this photograph, Lester Piggott's desperation clearly shows defeat in the 1970 Arc. Miss Dan finishes a creditable third

Mill Reef breaks the course record in the 1971 Prix de l'Arc de Triomphe, beating the filly Pistol Packer by three lengths. It was the climax to a well planned raid on Longchamp by Ian Balding

The 1974 One Thousand Guineas: some hats are already off for the Royal filly Highclere and Joe Mercer. No-one is sure, however, as Polygamy and Pat Eddery (near side) challenge relentlessly, and there was only a short head in it at the line

Above left 'The race of the century': the 1975 King George VI and Queen Elizabeth Diamond Stakes. The most gruelling race between two brave horses the author has ever described. Grundy takes Bustino on the shadow at the post after two pacemakers had made it the fastest mile-and-a-half race ever run at Ascot. *Right* The grey ghost Bruni, putting daylight between himself and his nearest pursuers to land the 1975 St Leger for Tony Murray and Captain Ryan Price

and over hurdles and he thoroughly understood how this extraordinarily intelligent horse needed to be handled. It was therefore a disaster when Jonjo broke his leg for a second time in a fall at Bangor-on-Dee, keeping him out for the whole of the 1980/1 season. Three days earlier he had won five out of six races at Wetherby and was at the peak of his form; now, Sea Pigeon was without a jockey.

Encouraged by the fact that Sea Pigeon had won the Champion Hurdle in 1980 without a race for the previous three months, Peter Easterby adopted a similar tactic for 1981. He sent Sea Pigeon south to contest the Holsten Diat Pils Hurdle at Sandown in November and, with both his stable jockeys involved at Wetherby on the same day, he engaged John Francome to ride.

It was first time out for Sea Pigeon, and John gave him a most sympathetic ride, biding his time until the entrance to the straight and then challenging Celtic Ryde to win by half a length. It was a perfect introduction to the season. Sea Pigeon's owner, Mr Pat Muldoon, was so clearly impressed with the way that John Francome had ridden that he asked him to ride his horse in the Champion Hurdle. A fortnight after Sandown, Sea Pigeon won the Bellway Fighting Fifth Hurdle at Newcastle. (He actually finished second to Bird's Nest, but was awarded the race after a Stewards' enquiry.)

The going was once again heavy for the National Hunt Festival, and without any commitment for Fred Winter's stable John Francome was free to ride Sea Pigeon. There were fourteen runners for the Waterford Crystal Champion Hurdle, including Bird's Nest, Pollardstown and Celtic Ryde. But Sea Pigeon was heavily supported in the ring and after opening at 11 to 4 he started a firm 7 to 4 favourite. For the first time for four years, Monksfield was missing from the line-up.

Even without Monksfield the race was run at a furious pace. Stan Mellor had purchased Meladon to act as pacemaker for Pollardstown, who had finished fifth and second in the race for the last two years. As Meladon blazed the trail, John Francome was conserving Sea Pigeon's energy, racing evenly and economically towards the rear. They crept closer at the fifth flight and were well in touch at the top of the hill. Swooping down to the third-last flight Pollardstown hit the front with Going Straight, Badsworth Boy and Daring Run on his heels, followed by the stable companions Starfen and Sea Pigeon.

For once, there was a change of scenery among the principals in the Champion Hurdle as they straightened up for the last flight. Now Ted Walsh on the Irish challenger Daring Run took over from Pollardstown, and when he jumped the last and maintained his narrow lead he must have been confident of winning, for Pollardstown was unable to find any more. Behind them John Francome was nursing Sea Pigeon. He had jumped the last flight a close third, but he understood Sea Pigeon and knew the need to wait for one decisive thrust; so he waited – and waited.

Half-way up the run-in Daring Run began to waver, and as Pollardstown began to find his second wind, John Francome played his ace. It was the ace of trumps, for Sea Pigeon quickened up and twenty-five yards from the post surged into the lead to win going away by a length and a half.

Sea Pigeon, now an eleven-year-old, had finished seventh in the Derby, was probably the 'classiest' horse ever to run under National Hunt rules, and joined Hatton's Grace as the oldest horses to have won the Champion Hurdle. For the second year running his Cheltenham win earned him the title of National Hunt Racehorse of the Year.

For sheer, calculating nerve it was the finest piece of race riding I have ever seen at Cheltenham. It was the sort of race that Charlie Smirke would have ridden, and it gave Sea Pigeon his second Hurdle Championship. After the race John Francome said: 'I just let the other two get on with it and then half-way up the hill I came and "did 'em" on the run-in. Sea Pigeon is the best hurdler I have ever sat on.'

Though we did not know it at the time, that was to be Sea Pigeon's last win. He broke a blood vessel attempting to win a record third Chester Cup, and in November he was beaten in the Fighting Fifth Hurdle at Newcastle. In February Peter Easterby tried to get him fit for another run at Cheltenham, but the old fire had gone and he was retired in 1982.

He has won more prize money than any other gelding to date, and his record represents one of the great training feats of all time. Sea Pigeon won sixteen flat races and twenty-one National Hunt races – thirty-seven in all – and he won £277,045 in stakes. He was turned out with his old stablemate and rival Night Nurse, and I have news that he is alive and well in blissful retirement on a farm at Slingsby.

John Francome had two rides and two wins on Sea Pigeon, watched by Jonjo O'Neill from the BBC Television commentary box at Cheltenham. Though understandably upset and emotional at the cruel act of fate that had deprived him of another Champion Hurdle, Jonjo paid John a most generous tribute for a job exceedingly well done. John added the Champion Hurdle to the Gold Cup he had won on Midnight Court. One of the most stylish of all Champion jockeys, he used to 'show jump' the fences, rather as Bryan Marshall had done in the fifties. There are distinct similarities in the way these two men presented their horses at a fence.

Fred Winter, for whom John Francome was stable jockey, referred to him as the best 'presenter' of a horse to a fence he had ever seen. John is a remarkably extrovert character. With his unruly mop of hair, his rich sense of humour and his irreverent attitude to authority, I for one was devastated when he returned to the weighing room after a fall at Chepstow on 9 April 1985 and announced his retirement. On the previous day he had ridden four winners at Huntingdon, which took him for the fifth time to a total of one hundred winners. In all, he rode 1138 winners – a record number.

In my time I have seen many great National Hunt jockeys. One of my pleasures in life on a day off from commentating is to walk down the course and stand at the second- or third-last fence to watch the steeplechases. Bryan Marshall was a marvel, always on the inside, timing his fences and arriving at the fence on an increasing stride – one-two-three-over. Tongue out, Bryan booting home another winner was a delight to see. Martin Molony in the same period was also a wizard in the saddle; his dash and skill were thrilling to watch from close quarters. I place John Francome in that same class. They all made it look so easy.

For power and drive in a finish there was no one to beat Fred Winter. The late Ryan Price said that Fred rode a hundred winners for him on which no other jockey could have won. I enjoyed watching the elegant style of Dick Francis; he was a perfect horseman, with beautiful 'hands'. William Robinson, who rode for Fulke Walwyn, was similar – always poised and with a flat-race finishing style. William is one of the few jockeys to have won the three major jumping races, the Grand National, the Gold Cup and the Champion Hurdle; Bryan Marshall, Bobby Beasley and Fred Winter are the others who in recent years have completed that glorious treble.

John Francome won the two Cheltenham races, but the Grand National eluded him, though he was second and third on Rough and Tumble in 1980 and 1979. So it was that John, after fifteen years of riding, retired to train and to write books. Racing is the poorer without his name in the number board.

CHELTENHAM, Wed. Mar. 14th 1979 (Heavy)
WATERFORD CRYSTAL CHAMPION HURDLE £22,730
2m 200yds

MONKSFIELD 7–12–0	DHughes	–1
Sea Pigeon (USA) 9–12–0	JJO'Neill	¾.2
Beacon Light 8–12–0	JFrancome	15.3
Within The Law 5–12–0	ABrown	6.4
Bird's Nest 9–12–0	ATurnell	7.5
Connaught Ranger 5–12–0	JBurke	10.6

S.P.: 9/4 MONKSFIELD, 4/1 Kybo, 6/1 Sea Pigeon, Western Rose, 10/1 Connaught Ranger, 13/1 Bird's Nest, 22/1 Beacon

Light, 40/1 Within The Law (Dr. M. Mangan) D. McDonogh. 10 Rn 4m 27.9

CHELTENHAM, Mar. 17th 1981 (Heavy)
WATERFORD CRYSTAL CHAMPION HURDLE CHALLENGE TROPHY (£32, 260: £9,805: £4,815: £2,320)
2m 3.30

SEA PIGEON (USA) 11–12–0	JFrancome	–1
Pollardstown 6–12–0	PBlacker	1½.2
Daring Run 6–12–0	MrTWalsh	nk.3
Starfen 5–12–0	MrTEasterby	7.4
Slaney Idol 6–12–0	PScudamore	8.5
Celtic Ryde 6–12–0	HDavies	2½.6
Bird's Nest 11–12–0	ATurnell	7
Going Straight 6–12–0	JPByrne	8
Heighlin 5–12–0	SJobar	9

S.P.: 7/4 SEA PIGEON, 6/1 Heighlin, 15/2 Celtic Ryde, 8/1 Daring Run, 9/1 Pollardstown, 11/1 Slaney Idol, 14/1 Starfen, 16/1 Bird's Nest. (P. Muldoon) M. H. Easterby, Great Habton, Yorks. 14 Rn 4m 11.40

1980
Spillers Stewards Cup

Repetitious

While driving down to Goodwood on the day before the Stewards Cup, as I was passing Fontwell Park racecourse I had the sensation of the road ahead moving alarmingly in waves. I took the first turning to the right, drove on for a few hundred yards and was just conscious enough to pull in to the verge, switch off the engine and open the car door. I fell out of the car almost into a gateway and rolled another twenty feet into a grass field. I was then extremely and violently sick and I passed out on the grass. I lay there for five hours, and though the car door was open and I was in the field flat out, no one stopped and I did not have the strength to call for help when I heard someone passing.

I simply did not know what was wrong or from what I was suffering, except that there had been an identical happening whilst driving back from York in July. There I had found a lay-by and had endured these identical symptoms of acute nausea. On that occasion I had recovered sufficiently to get myself to a hotel in Doncaster, and the following day I was just well enough to continue my journey. Now, here I was again in exactly the same predicament. I was due to check in at Goodwood with my preview on the Stewards Cup, but as the time drew up to five o'clock that deadline was impossible and I was in absolutely no condition to preview anything. I managed to get back into the car, and somehow I drove to the nearest telephone box and reported in to the BBC Sports Room.

I succeeded in getting to Ryan Price's doctor, John Chard, whose later death from cancer was a terrible blow to all his devoted patients. John detected the smell of petrol on my clothes and at first we thought that I had been inhaling petrol fumes through a loose pipe. The car was immediately suspect number one, and the manufacturers sent an identical replacement down within forty-eight hours. Meanwhile, I was still feeling terribly ill. Joanna, my wife, came down and the following day, though I was still very wobbly at the knees and had a terrible headache, she drove me to Goodwood to commentate on the Stewards Cup.

I was feeling ghastly. My eyes were not able to focus properly and, dosed up with analgesics to stem the hammering headache that still remained, my reactions were dulled. I was not looking forward to coping with the Stewards Cup, this year with twenty-eight runners. But the show must go on, so I began my preparation. Even as I worked in the small radio control room behind the new commentary box, the mist which had shrouded the course now became thick sea fret and visibility was down to a hundred yards. Not even the television cameras could penetrate the fog, and the two early races took place in total silence without any public address commentary.

We heard that the Stewards Cup had started, and I peered through the mist. After what seemed like an eternity, ghost-like figures emerged and flashed past the post. This was no time for finesse. I latched on to three horses – Repetitious, Eagle Boy and Sovereign Rose. These were the only three words I uttered, but I said them several times over so that my faithful producer John Fenton could write them down. It was in fact a photo finish, and in due course the result matched the three that I had given out; strangely, there was no fourth horse announced.

Several minutes later the Judge, Michael Hancock, appeared at the back of the commentary box and asked Peter O'Sullevan and me if we knew what had finished fourth. Neither of us did, but by a process of elimination after studying the photograph we agreed on Sparkling Boy, who was officially placed fourth by a committee comprising two commentators and the Judge. Sparkling

Boy's owner collected £1748, thanks to our combined efforts.

For once, I was more than grateful for the fog, for I would never have been able to cope with the normal cavalry charge, which is a pretty severe test even for a commentator in full possession of his faculties.

The week passed and I gradually shook off what transpired to be a severe case of inhaling exhaust fumes, caused by a leaking exhaust pipe in conjunction with a welding fault in the bodywork. When the sunshine roof was open in a certain position it was sucking the exhaust fumes into the cabin, and I had been filling my lungs with carbon monoxide.

GOODWOOD, Jul. 29th 1980

SPILLERS STEWARDS' CUP H'CAP (Listed Race) £24,524
(£7,442: £3,646: £1,748) 6f 3.10

REPETITIOUS 3–7–2	AClark	–1
Eagle Boy 4–7–4	ANesbitt	s.hd.2
Sovereign Rose 3–8–10	WCarson	¾.3
Sparkling Boy 3–7–8	DMcKay	nk.4
Standaan (FR) 4–9–1	LPiggott	hd.5
Queens Pride 4–7–8	JLowe	¾.6
Escovitch 4–8–8	RSidebottom	s.hd.7
Gamblers Dream 3–7–8	KDarley	nk.8
Davenport Boy 4–8–4	JReid	hd.9
Pace Jean 3–8–7	GStarkey	10

S.P.: 11/2 Sovereign Rose, 9/1 Cree Song, 10/1 Miss Pudge, Overtrick, Pace Jean, 12/1 Primula Boy, Queens Pride, 15/1 REPETITIOUS, Davenport Boy, 16/1 Artipiar, 20/1 Sparkling Boy, Standaan, 25/1 Escovitch, 28/1 Pink Blues, 33/1 Eagle Boy. (Mrs A. M. Trimble) G. Harwood, Pullborough, Sussex. 28 Rn 1m 12.36

1981
Sun Grand National

Aldaniti

The victory of the previously crippled Aldaniti, ridden by Bob Champion, in the 1981 *Sun* Grand National has been well chronicled. Jonathan Powell's moving book *Champion's Story* re-tells a truly monumental tale. It is a story of loyalty, pain and suffering, guts and determination, and of triumph against the odds; a story of winners – two of them – Aldaniti and Bob Champion.

In 1979, when Bob Champion was diagnosed as suffering from cancer, he was stable jockey to Josh Gifford and had already made a name for himself as a first-class horseman, much in demand. It did not seem possible for him ever to resume that career, but throughout his long and harrowing treatment, he had one priceless target for which to aim. He had such faith in a young horse that he had ridden, Aldaniti, that he believed that one day the horse would win the Grand National.

Jonathan Powell's book brings into sharp relief the exceptional loyalty that Josh Gifford showed in helping Bob Champion back in his career, and the extraordinary faith that Aldaniti's owners Mr and Mrs Nick Embiricos had in their chaser. It was later made into a highly successful film, *Champions*.

Strangely, racing films are not generally box-office hits, but once I had got over the shock of seeing Josh Gifford portrayed by Edward Woodward I was extremely moved by the full horrendous story of Bob Champion's fight to regain his health and fitness. It was a wonderful film, full of sadness and joy and mounting to a heroic climax in the 1981 *Sun* Grand National. At the film's preview, which I was fortunate enough to be able to attend, the atmosphere was astonishingly emotional and affected virtually everyone present.

Aldaniti

On three occasions when it seemed that Aldaniti was about to become a top-class chaser, he was injured. Each time, he returned to his owner's Barkfold Manor Stud in Sussex, where rest and loving care brought him back to fitness. During Aldaniti's interrupted racing career he had shown that Bob Champion's prophecy (made on dismounting after winning at Leicester in November 1977) – that one day he would win the Grand National – had a sound foundation. Nevertheless, in that year Aldaniti had a disastrous run in the Hennessy Gold Cup when he finished third to Bachelor's Hall after making a comprehensive mistake at the second fence. On his return to Findon he was found to be lame and it was later diagnosed that he had chipped a bone, so it was back to Barkfold Manor.

In 1979 Aldaniti returned to training and ran a marvellous third in the Gold Cup behind Alverton; he was then a slightly unlucky loser of the Scottish Grand National, beaten on the run-in by Fighting Fit. Aldaniti ended the season by winning a minor race at Sandown, and he had shown Josh Gifford that he was indeed a National horse. Then Bob Champion was found to be suffering from cancer, and at the start of the 1979/80 season Aldaniti broke down during a race at Sandown. Josh could have been forgiven for thinking that this dream of glory at Aintree was fast becoming a nightmare. For Bob was now admitted to the Royal Marsden Hospital for painful chemotherapy treatment, while Aldaniti returned to Barkfold Manor yet again. In *My Greatest Training Triumph* by Peter Watson and John Hughes. Josh has related the Aldaniti story. He thought at this time that Aldaniti's injury was so bad that the horse might have to be put down. He recounts:

. . . But Aldaniti's owners are different. I knew they wouldn't consider anything like that; they would want to take him home and give him every possible chance . . . they would look after him. I was convinced he would never run again.

On 22 December 1980 Aldaniti came back to Findon and went into training, with the Grand National as his primary objective. Josh Gifford rode him in all his work and slowly the horse began to regain his old form. From *My Greatest Training Triumph*, Josh continues:

Everything went perfectly, I could hardly believe it. The more work we did, the better his legs seemed to be. He was beginning to go very well and lose his tummy and it then became a question of picking the right race for him before the National.

The race Josh chose was the Whitbread Trial at Ascot on 11 February 1981, and few who watched that race had any doubt that here, indeed, was a National horse. He jumped brilliantly and won, as he liked, by four lengths.

Aldaniti was not the only recovered invalid to return to Findon, for Bob Champion had won his lonely fight – he was officially declared clear of cancer in November 1980, and took up his old job again. Obtaining rides was not easy, but the breakthrough came at Ascot on 13 December 1980 when he won the SGB Chase on Henry Bishop and followed up by winning the next race on Kybo. A double was exactly what had been required at that moment. I was delighted to be able to interview Bob after this remarkable double in the radio studio at Ascot for *Sport on Two*, and he revealed that he had been treated for cancer but was now clear and that this was the best tonic he could wish for.

So, when Aldaniti returned to win the Whitbread Trial, Bob Champion was in the saddle. When the weights came out for the National, Aldaniti had been given 10 stone 13lb. Josh by-passed Cheltenham and went all out for Aintree.

So far, the Aintree meeting was not going well either for Mr and Mrs Nick Embiricos or for Bob Champion. On the opening day of the meeting in the Topham Trophy their chaser Stonepark was killed after breaking his neck at the first fence, which was particularly distressing for them on the eve of the National. Bob Champion was also in some pain and discomfort after a heavy fall in his last race on Kilbroney. He had been kicked in the back by another runner when he fell at the water jump. It seemed an ill omen at the time.

Anyone who has not made the pilgrimage to Aintree to see the work-outs on the morning of the Grand National has missed the most enjoyable and good-natured preview of any big race. Everyone is there – officials, stewards, owners, trainers, jockeys, press, television, visiting 'firemen' from the USA; there is usually a smattering of stetsons and, of course, the big-race candidates, identified only by the trainers' initials on the rugs. It is hard to know who is who, but information is shared and passed on in the most amicable way. After Bob Champion had ridden Aldaniti at a canter he was besieged by well-wishers when he dismounted, and I thought at the time how remarkably composed and confident he was as he signed autographs, was interviewed for radio and television and spoke to everyone. Bob was able to reassure us that the injury to his back had responded to treatment and that he was completely fit.

This year there were two very human themes which the press and broadcasting media had highlighted: Bob Champion's return from the scourge of cancer, and the demanding privations that John Thorne had undergone to shed two stone in weight in order to ride his horse Spartan Missile.

The Race

On perfect going, thirty-nine horses faced the tapes at 3.20p.m. on a glorious sunny afternoon; three minutes later they were streaming away from the stands across the Melling Road to the first of the twenty-eight fences. It is a long run to the first, and with such a large field many horses take a strong hold and approach the fence too fast. Bob Champion had a moment of extreme anxiety here when Aldaniti stood back a stride too far and landed heavily; his legs buckled with the shock of impact and he was very nearly a faller. Fortunately, this story runs for another nine and a half minutes – Aldaniti recovered his balance and went after the next fence.

In a remarkable interview in the *Sunday People* given by Bob Champion to the paper's racing correspondent Jonathan Powell, he revealed with astonishing candour just what winning the National meant to him.

> I badly want to win the race for so many people, in particular the doctors and nurses who kept me going when all hope seemed gone. I also want to win for Josh who kept my job waiting for me and then helped me through a bad patch when the horses were wrong and my confidence was rock bottom. Few, if any, trainers would have done the same. My family, friends and many owners were terrific too. Nick and Valda Embiricos sent me get well cards and I even had one from Aldaniti who had his own fan club organised by their daughter Alexandra.
>
> But most of all I want to win the Grand National for all the patients still in hospital. If any success I have can give people a fresh heart and just a bit of hope then everything that has happened to me in the past twenty months will have been worthwhile.

To have fallen at the first fence would have been an unmitigated disaster. Bob had accurately forecast that Aldaniti's bold jumping could give him problems in those early fences, and they were, in fact, to fall at the first fence the following year.

Gradually Aldaniti got his eye in and he jumped with a stronger sense of self-preservation. He had never fallen and now he began to respect the fences. At the Canal Turn, Bob Champion found that Aldaniti's quick and accurate jumping had carried him up to the leaders, and at Valentines (the twin jump for Bechers Brook,) Bob found himself leading the field, embarrassingly early and certainly not according to plan.

As the field came back across the Melling Road there was Aldaniti with his white face, and Bob Champion in those now so distinctive colours – white with the blue sash and blue armbands and blue cap – bowling along thoroughly enjoying themselves. I was worried at the time that Bob might have played his hand too soon, but by the manner in which Aldaniti jumped the Chair fence and then the water jump and then scurried round the turn, it was obvious Bob still had plenty of horse under him.

In the commentary box Lord Oaksey, who has shared many Grand National broadcasts with me, watched on the television monitor as Aldaniti jumped his way towards Bechers for the second time. The television roving eye kept station with Bob, and Aldaniti seemed like an Olympic hurdler, programmed to take just so many strides between fences. He was fluent and majestic, and at that moment it did appear as if some outside force had taken over, for both horse and rider seemed inspired.

John and I held our breath for Bechers, with its yawning chasm on the landing side. Here Aldaniti was bold – almost too bold, for the drop nearly caught him out and those legs buckled and for a brief moment the hopes and dreams of his rider hung once again in the balance. At this moment of crisis the horseman took over, and Bob picked up Aldaniti by instinct. Not for nothing was he the son of a famous huntsman with a pedigree going back for seven generations of professional huntsmen.

Aldaniti galloped relentlessly on, but at the Canal Turn Bob could now hear his nearest pursuers, who were the 1979 winner Rubstic, Royal Mail, Three to One, and Senator Maclacury. As the field came back across the Melling Road Aldaniti was still in front, but Philip Blacker, now a distinguished horse sculptor, was laying down a formidable challenge on the New Zealand-bred Royal Mail; however, a mistake at the second-last fence put paid to their hopes.

As the last fence approached Bob knew that he had a very tired horse under him and he jumped the fence sluggishly; it was going to take a prodigious effort to keep Aldaniti galloping. The nightmare of Crisp was going through the rider's mind as he reached the elbow, with 'the longest furlong in the world' in front of him.

We in the stands could see that John Thorne, who had come from a long way back after the Melling Road, was getting a tremendous response from Spartan Missile, now running on through the pursuers. At the elbow he appeared a very real threat to Bob Champion's dreams, and a classic finish was then enacted in a climax which had the crowd evenly divided in their loyalties. I am sure, as the roar of the crowd swelled to fantastic proportions, that just as many were rooting for the fifty-four-year-old owner, breeder, trainer and jockey of Spartan Missile as were for Aldaniti and Bob Champion.

Bob Champion, the true professional, kept his head. It is easy to see now where his inspiration came from: he was, after all, riding for all the cancer patients still in hospital – he was going to win for them and he was not going to be beaten now. The tiredness vanished as he drove Aldaniti out to the finish, and this brave and lovely horse kept up the gallop to the end. Spartan Missile could do no more. In the commentary box we just could not believe it; we were now describing a fairy tale come true. With as emotional a summary as I can remember, John and I, tears streaming down our cheeks, did our best to describe the most impossible of all happenings – the triumphal victory in this most searching of athletic contests of two one-time virtual cripples, the one human and the other equine. Nor did John forget to pay most eloquent tribute to the runner-up, his friend John Thorne, who, like Lord Oaksey, had come so close to realising his greatest ambition – to win the National.

Aintree erupted, and there was hardly a dry eye in the place as a smiling Bob Champion sat astride the chestnut with the white face, flanked by two mounted policemen. The Grand National has provided us in recent years with some dramatic moments, but the atmosphere that day was more highly charged with emotion than any I can remember.

LIVERPOOL, Sat., Apr. 4th 1981 (Good)
SUN GRAND NATIONAL H'CAP CHASE £51,324
(£15,612: £7,676: £3,828) 4m 4f 3.20

ALDANITI 11–10–13 RChampion –1

Spartan Missile 9–11–5	MrMJThorne	4.2
Royal Mail (NZ) 11–11–7	PBlacker	2.3
Three to One 10–10–3	MrRTGDun	nk.4
Senator MacLacury 7–10–2	JPHarty	12.5
Royal Exile (USA) 12–10–0	BdeHaan	5.6
Rubstic 12–10–7	MBarnes	7
Coolishall 12–10–3	WSmith	8
Rathlek 11–10–1	PBarton	9
So 12–10–8	JFrancome	10
Sebastian V 13–10–2	RLamb	11
Cheers 9–10–0	PScudamore	12

S.P.: 8/1 Spartan Missile, 10/1 ALDANITI, 11/1 Rubstic, 14/1 Zongalero, 16/1 Kylogue Lady, Royal Exile, Royal Mail, Royal Stuart, 20/1 Cheers, S MacLacury, Vintner, 25/1 Coolishall. (N. Embiricos) J. Gifford, Findon, Sussex. 39 Rn 9m 47.20

1981
Derby

Shergar

The appalling fate that befell the Aga Khan's stallion Shergar, who was stolen from his stud and has never been heard of since, makes his runaway victory seem that much more poignant. Though many will remember the Derby that he won so decisively, for me it was a ghastly day that I recall with absolutely no pleasure.

So as to be near at hand for the early morning radio previews from the course on the morning of the Derby, I stayed overnight at a hotel near Chobham. After a walk on the Downs at the crack of dawn, I returned to the hotel for breakfast. Time was becoming short and I hurriedly checked out and set off for Epsom to avoid the inevitable traffic jam.

Just before the *Daily Mirror* Handicap, the race before the Derby, I fished into my briefcase for my clear race-reading spectacles, but to my horror the case was empty. In the bright sunshine I had been wearing sunglasses all the time; but they are not suitable for reading a race as the heavy tint destroys the colours. Usually I keep a spare pair of spectacles in the car, but, panic, I was not in my own car – that was being serviced and I was driving a hired car. I obviously must have left my clear spectacles back at the hotel. There was certainly no time to go and collect them before the Derby. I was going to have to improvise.

There were twelve runners for the *Daily Mirror* Handicap and I felt distinctly uneasy, but I managed without my spectacles and just used the large binoculars for most of the race, slipping the sunglasses down from the top of my head for the last furlong. I got lucky, for

Shergar helped me out. He took the lead at Tattenham Corner and he just went further and further ahead with every stride. For once, the Derby was a one-horse race and Shergar came home by an easy ten lengths. 'You'll need a telescope to see the rest', I remember saying in my commentary, though actually my own spectacles would have done better.

My spectacles were found in the hotel room and I collected them on the way home. 'We wondered how you were managing without them,' said the receptionist. 'With great difficulty', I replied. I hate to think what might have happened if there had been a really eventful finish to that Derby, with a challenger coming from a long way back in the field, as had happened when Troy won in 1979.

EPSOM, Wed., Jun. 3rd 1981 (Soft)
DERBY STAKES (Gr 1) £149,900 1½m

SHERGAR 9–0	WRSwinburn	–1
Glint of Gold 9–0	JMatthias	10.2
Scintillating Air 9–0	GBaxter	2.3
Shotgun 9–0	LPiggott	2.4
Church Parade 9–0	WCarson	4.5
Sheer Grit 9–0	JMercer	1½.6
Silver Season 9–0	EJohnson	1.7
Riberetto 9–0	PEddery	hd.8
Sunley Builds 9–0	PWaldron	4.9
King's General 9–0	BTaylor	3.10

S.P.: 10/11 Shergar, 7/1 Shotgun, 11/1 Kalaglow, 13/1 Glint of Gold, 16/1 Al Nasr, 22/1 Riberetta, 25/1 Church Parade, Kind of Hush, 28/1 Robellino, Sheer Grit, 50/1 Scintillating Air.
(Aga Khan) M. Stoute, Newmarket. 18 Rn 2m 44.21

1984
Whitbread Gold Cup

Special Cargo

Sandown Park is a fine viewing course with the Grandstand built on the side of a hill, and the running can be seen from all parts of the Members' Lawn and the floor of Tattersalls. The line of seven fences – two plain, an open ditch, the water and three taken in quick succession by the railway embankment – provides a superb spectacle when watched from the hill. Sandown is very popular, but it has one drawback. The course finishes for the hurdle and steeplechase converge towards the winning post – there are in fact two winning posts, one for each course, and the angle can prove very deceptive, particularly if the horses are racing wide apart. The 1984 Whitbread Gold Cup was to provide a conundrum which only the Judge with the aid of the photo finish could solve. It was one of the most exciting finishes I can remember for the Whitbread, or, indeed, any race at Sandown.

The Whitbread Gold Cup was the first sponsored race to be run in Britain. It is run late in the season in April, as the only National Hunt race in a high-class flat-race card. The meeting draws huge crowds and the Whitbread frequently steals the thunder of the other races. In 1984 that was most certainly the case, and the air was electric when the Judges' announcer said, 'Photograph'.

That year's race seemed to be a direct confrontation between the two leading trainers Michael Dickinson and Fred Winter. They were involved in a long drawn-out duel for the title of leading trainer, and if either won it would certainly clinch the championship. Dickinson was represented by Ashley House, the 7 to 2 joint favourite, and Lettoch, whose price was 11 to 2, and Winter by the other joint favourite Plundering.

Fulke Walwyn, who had sent out the winner six times, was relying on two horses who were making a comeback after injury. One was Diamond Edge, who was a handsome, quality chaser and had won the Whitbread in 1979 and 1981 and come fourth in 1982. Diamond Edge had won the twenty-fifth running of the Whitbread in April 1981 and, without a race in between, the twenty-fifth anniversary race for the Hennessy Gold Cup at Newbury in November – a quite astonishing feat of training by the master of Saxon House. After the 1982 Whitbread the horse suffered leg trouble and missed the whole of the next season. He reappeared at the age of thirteen at the 1984 National Hunt Festival in the Cathcart Challenge Cup, when he finished third. This was in fact his preparation race for another crack at the Whitbread, to try for a record third win.

Fulke Walwyn's other representative was the Queen Mother's Sandown specialist Special Cargo, another ex-invalid who had broken down twice. He was fired, and then underwent an operation for a carbon-fibre implant into the tendon. Following this successful operation he was off the course for two years before returning to win the Grand Military Gold Cup in March 1984. That was his fourth win at Sandown and in winning his next race at Lingfield he provided Bill Smith with his five-hundredth winner.

Bill Smith told me that there was never really any question as to whether he would partner Diamond Edge or Special Cargo. He did, of course, have the choice as stable jockey, but he regarded one as a Gold Cup horse who had already won two Whitbreads and the other as a tip-top handicapper; so he rode Diamond Edge in what was to be his last ride before retiring.

The Race

Her Majesty the Queen Mother has long been a staunch supporter of National Hunt racing. To begin with her horses were trained by Peter Cazalet at Fairlawne in Kent, and on his death in May 1973 they were transferred to Fulke Walwyn at Lambourn. The story of the Queen Mother's steeplechasing ownership is beautifully told in Bill Curling's book *Royal Champion: The Story of Steeplechasing's First Lady*. This tells the story of over 330 winners and includes such well-known chasers as Monaveen, Devon Loch, who came within 100 yards of winning the Grand National, The Rip, Makaldar and Game Spirit. Publication of the book coincided with the Queen Mother's eightieth birthday in August 1980.

From the book I learnt that Special Cargo had been bought by Fulke Walwyn as a five-year-old at the Doncaster Sales in 1978 after winning a 'bumper' in Ireland three months earlier. After a long rest, Special Cargo won the Grand Military Gold Cup at Sandown in March 1984, ridden by Fulke Walwyn's assistant, Mr Gerald Oxley. For the Whitbread Kevin Mooney was in the saddle.

On extremely fast ground Diamond Edge took command of proceedings from the start. Jumping fluently and accurately, he led the field on the first circuit. Bill Smith said that Diamond Edge was the most brilliant jumper he had ever ridden.

> He was a very bold, free horse and attacked the fences and though he would occasionally leave one out and take it low, he never felt as if he was going to fall. He was the quickest jumper I ever sat on, and on that day at Sandown he had never jumped more brilliantly; he was like quicksilver.

Early in the race the Dickinson horse Lettoch had been badly hampered when Donegal Prince fell at the third fence on the downhill run to the Eclipse start. He lost his place, but gradually fought back into contention on the second circuit and running to the Pond fence, the third from home, he took the lead from Diamond Edge. Plundering, who had always been in the leading group, was still there with a chance but Special Cargo had begun to lose his place as they jumped the three railway fences, and appeared out of the race.

As the three leaders raced towards the last fence it seemed as if there were three different possibilities for the climax to the Whitbread; Lettoch could hold on and give Dickinson the trainer's title; Plundering could stage a rally and make Fred Winter champion; or Diamond Edge, fighting back like a tiger, could make history by winning for the third time. At this stage Special Cargo, a poor fourth, did not enter into calculations.

Lettoch landed first, but Bill Smith was hanging up his boots that night and he found his old friend and ally Diamond Edge responding to his calls as Plundering began to weaken. From the commentary box it now looked like Lettoch versus Diamond Edge, and this desperate set-to had the crowds roaring. Few, I suspect, were at this stage watching Special Cargo; I certainly wasn't, and just when I thought that Diamond Edge had headed Lettoch twenty yards from the post, Lettoch got his head back in front again. What happened then was unbelievable, and even seeing the action replay it still seems impossible. Special Cargo, having jumped the last fence in fourth place and seemingly out of it, now began to run on up the stands side. He had so much ground to make up that it looked a forlorn hope, but Kevin Mooney rode a flat-race finish and the three horses – Lettoch, Diamond Edge and Special Cargo – flashed past the post together, with Special Cargo finishing faster than anything. Had the Royal horse got there in time? No one knew for certain, because of the notorious angle.

Sandown now witnessed a stampede as racegoers surged towards the winners' enclosure. There was a tremendous cheer when the result was announced – first Special Cargo, second Lettoch, and third Diamond Edge. I thought that the roof would come in. Everything about this race was remarkable: it was the fastest Whitbread ever run; two short heads separated the first three home; and Special Cargo was the Queen Mother's most important winner – he had come back from a serious injury to run the race of his life. It was Kevin Mooney's biggest winner and Fulke Walwyn's seventh success in the race, and it was Special Cargo's fifth win at Sandown; he had not been beaten in five appearances there.

I felt the greatest sympathy for Bill Smith. He had come within a few inches of riding the Whitbread winner for the third time and making history on Diamond Edge. Years later he told me that if he could ride the race again, he would not do anything differently. Diamond Edge had won his race with Lettoch, just twenty-five yards short of the post, and had run magnificently.

Far from being depressed at his agonisingly narrow defeat, Bill was lifted by the tremendous enthusiasm now being shown by the crowd around the unsaddling enclosure. The Queen Mother still looked surprised as she received the Whitbread trophy herself, instead of presenting it as had been arranged. Never has there been a more popular winner of a major jumping prize. Bill was invited to the Royal Box, where the Queen Mother made him feel that he had won the race, as over a glass of champagne they watched a re-run on the television monitor. He will certainly never forget his last ride.

Special Cargo, his 'carbon-fibre legs' holding up well, returned to Sandown again and won two more Grand Military Gold Cups, making his record in that race three wins in three years. At the age of fourteen he tried again in 1987, but could finish only fourth to his old rival Burnt Oak.

As for Bill Smith, he retired to breed horses, to help manage the Maktoum empire, and to talk so knowledgeably about jumping on BBC Television. The following week as a 'civilian' he went to Newmarket for the Two Thousand Guineas, where everyone who spoke to him remarked on the thrilling finish to the Whitbread, and he began to realise that although he had not won, he had taken part in what will always be regarded as a steeplechasing classic. One racegoer even said: 'What a fantastic coup you must all have had, put in to make the running for the Queen Mother's horse.'

SANDOWN, Sat., Apr. 28th 1984 (Firm)
WHITBREAD GOLD CUP HANDICAP CHASE (Listed Race)
£25,472 3m 5f

SPECIAL CARGO 11–2	KMooney	–1
Lettoch 7–10–12	REarnshaw	s.hd.2
Diamond Edge 13–11–7	WSmith	s.hd.3
Plundering 7–10–3	BdeHaan	1½.4
Skegby 10–10–9	MBrennan	4.5
Kudos 9–10–0	DDutton	6

S.P.: 7/2 Ashley House, Plundering, 11/2 SPECIAL CARGO, Lettoch, Diamond Edge, 25/1 Skegby, 33/1 Kudos. (Queen Elizabeth The Queen Mother) F. Walwyn, Lambourn. 13 Rn

Lester Piggott

The riding career of Lester Piggott runs through my span of commentating like a golden thread. He has provided me with some magnificent moments to describe and I could quite easily have filled this book with memorable races that all involved him. In addition, Lester played an important part in the beginning of my own career.

In March 1954 I was summoned to Hurst Park racecourse by Reg Moore, who was the head of the British Amplifying and Recording Company (BRARCO), which supplied the public address system to most British racecourses. They also provided the announcers and, more recently, the race commentator after this was introduced first at Goodwood and later on other racecourses.

As the running commentary became universally accepted, thanks largely to the skill and technique of the early exponents, Bob Haynes and Michael Seth-Smith, more courses were asking for the service and there was a vacancy for another commentator on the panel. So, armed with my binoculars, I attended Hurst Park racecourse on 6 March 1954 to find that there was another would-be commentator there as well. We divided up the card and did test commentaries on tape on alternate races.

One of my races was the Triumph Hurdle, which produced one of the biggest gambles of the season when Prince Charlemagne, a high-class three-year-old who had run in the Derby and the Two Thousand Guineas, was backed from 5 to 1 down to 11 to 4 favourite, even though he had never before run in a hurdle race. He was ridden that day by Lester Piggott. As hurdle races go it was pretty easy to describe, for Prince Charlemagne took the lead at half-way, went clear and, despite flattening the last flight of hurdles, won unchallenged by six lengths to land the gamble.

I knew that my races had gone reasonably well, but I did not know how the other chap had fared. He turned out to be Lt-Col. Tony Cooke, late of the 9th Lancers, who seemed to know everything there was to know about racing. I was not particularly hopeful of my chances. So I was delighted to receive a request for a further trial, this time at Sandown on the following Saturday. One of the races was the twenty-six-runner Imperial Cup, won by the 20 to 1 chance The Pills. Lester Piggott rode the 4 to 1 favourite Noholme, but this time he never featured.

Tony Cooke and I were both taken on to the panel although there was only one vacancy; we got half a job each, and I was let loose on an unwary public shortly afterwards at Plumpton. Tony Cooke later became the ITV race commentator and had a distinguished career in television.

But back to Lester Piggott, who was not only the most superb judge of pace, timing and tactics, he also knew his way around the form book. Consequently he had an uncanny knack of being on the right horse at the right time. I was once admonished by one of the truly great characters in racing, the trainer 'Monty' Smyth, who buttonholed me one day shortly after I had been over-praising Piggott for a race that he had won. Monty said: 'You do go on about that Piggott fellow. Remember, Peter, he can't come without the horse.'

Point taken, but even so, many of Piggott's big-race wins were memorable, and there were plenty of them. Raymond Glendenning covered the first three of Piggott's Derby wins, on Never Say Die, Crepello and St Paddy; then came Sir Ivor, Nijinsky, Roberto, Empery, The Minstrel and Teenoso.

Two of those were desperate, bloodcurdling affairs. Roberto received the full Piggott treatment to get up to short head Rheingold, and had a very hard race. The Minstrel also ran on most bravely under some fearsome whip-cracks to beat Hot Grove by a neck. These races saw Piggott at his most awesome, where his determination was totally overpowering and the horse just seemed to have no option but to stretch out its head and win.

After the close finish on Roberto, Piggott did not ride into the winners' enclosure but dismounted out on the course, and he walked through to the weighing room without a cheer from the crowd. No one knew for sure which horse had won – the two finishers had been racing very close – and there followed a twenty-minute Stewards' enquiry, at the end of which Rheingold turned out to be the offender, but retained second place.

The British concern for fair play had been violated when the Australian jockey Bill Williamson had been unceremoniously 'jocked off' Roberto on the grounds that he had not fully recovered from an injury. Whether Bill would have won is something we will never know, but the crowd showed its feelings when he won the next race, the Woodcote Stakes, and he came back to a Derby winner's reception.

Sir Ivor's last-furlong swoop was dramatic and effective, but even Lester must have experienced a moment of panic when the colt hung fire when he was asked to quicken two furlongs from the finish. On Nijinsky Lester rode a sympathetic and gentle race, which is described in the section on that great horse. Empery's win gave Lester great satisfaction, for it was his seventh Derby and he beat the record held jointly by Steve Donoghue and Jem Robinson. His last win in the race, on Teenoso, was the easiest of his record nine successes in the Blue Riband of the turf.

1984 proved to be a significant year for Lester Piggott. In the twilight of his career he was close to taking yet another record, that of twenty-seven Classic wins, set by Frank Buckle between 1792 and 1827. In the Gold Seal Oaks, in the first year of the race's sponsorship, he had equalled that record of 27 wins on Circus Plume. Now for the St Leger, which he had already won seven times but for which he was without a ride. Then late in the day it was announced that he would be replacing the stable jockey, American Darrel McHargue, on Commanche Run, trained by Luca Cumani. With McHargue under suspension, Lester had already ridden Commanche Run to win the March Stakes at Goodwood, and the decision to engage him to ride in the St Leger was taken by the owner, Singapore trainer Ivan Allen. So, not for the first time, there was controversy over Lester's big-race mount. I considered that Commanche Run had a really tough opponent in Baynoun, owned by the Aga Khan. Baynoun had won the Geoffrey Freer Stakes at Newbury and looked an ideal St Leger type; furthermore, he was to be ridden by Steve Cauthen.

Also in the field of twelve were three horses trained by Guy Harwood: Alphabatim, who had been disappointing when Lester Piggott had ridden him into fifth place in the Derby, and who had finished three lengths second to Baynoun at Newbury; Crazy, who had won the Tote Ebor with 8 stone 13 lb; and a pacemaker, Librate. I have selected this 1984 St Leger as my most memorable Lester Piggott race, for not only was it one of his greatest rides, it also made turf history.

1984 Holsten Pils St Leger – *Commanche Run*

Librate led for a mile, but Lester Piggott always had Commanche Run in close touch lying second; at the entrance to the long four-and-a-half-furlong straight, Lester sent him into the lead. Shernazar, the half-brother to Shergar, was in pursuit and then came Baynoun ridden by Steve Cauthen. All the way up the straight Lester kept quickening the pace and he was hard at work on Commanche Run fully two furlongs from the post, at which point Baynoun began a long, steady challenge which threatened, although I never thought he would get past Commanche Run. Baynoun kept on responding as Steve Cauthen rode his hardest, but Lester had a half-length lead and, riding at full strength as if his life depended on the outcome, he kept that lead to the post to win by a neck.

It was as powerful a finish as he has ever ridden, and to this day I am still not sure just how Baynoun was beaten for he did not flinch but kept running on bravely to the end with the utmost resolution. After the race Luca Cumani said that Darrel McHargue would have won on the horse. I am not so sure. Even though the American had ridden 405 winners in one year in the States, he had not impressed me with his riding here. This was a vintage ride by Piggott, and he received a tremendous reception both as he rode in and at the presentation of the ridiculous hat that the Doncaster executive gives to the winning rider of the St Leger. The Doncaster manager, Don Cox, an ex-racing correspondent himself, did no favours for the waiting pressmen who wished to interview Lester: he unlocked the back door of the jockeys' changing room and Lester slipped out unnoticed – an unworthy and perhaps rather tawdry anti-climax to a day when racing history was made on Town Moor.

Royal Ascot

Lester Piggott was a standard feature of Royal Ascot, being top or joint top rider eighteen times, and together they have produced some memorable occasions over the past twenty-eight years. Lester has won 110 races at the Royal meeting, 11 winners of the Gold Cup, 7 Cork and Orrery Stakes, 7 Chesham and 7 Norfolk Stakes, 6 King's Stand and 6 Jersey Stakes, 5 Queen Anne Stakes, 5 Coronation Stakes, 5 St James's Palace Stakes and 5 Hardwick Stakes, 4 Ascot Vases and 4 Royal Hunt Cups – the list is endless. It is a record that is never likely to be surpassed.

One of the features of his riding career is the length of time for which he was at the top, and nor did his ability taper off for he was as effective in the last years of his career as he had been in the fifties and sixties. Nowhere was his cool, calculating confidence more apparent than in the bubbling cauldron of atmosphere and high tension that is Royal Ascot. Lester always seemed so unaffected by the pressure, and performed there with calm and ruthless efficiency.

He also rode seven winners of the King George VI and Queen Elizabeth Stakes run in July, and always seemed to excel on the short, uphill run-in at Ascot. So, also, did he at Goodwood, the most difficult of courses to master; and round the turns at Chester, riding American 'acey-duecey' style (the inside stirrup leather shorter than the outside one), he had an incomparable record. Then there are the big races that he won at York, which I believe with the July course at Newmarket were his favourite tracks. Add to this his remarkable record abroad where he rode 822 winners and you will realise why it was uncommonly difficult to chose one race as the most memorable.

HURST PARK, Mar. 6th 1954 (Good)
TRIUMPH HURDLE £1370 2m 3.0

PRINCE CHARLEMAGNE 10–10	LPiggott	–1
Syrte 11–0	REmery	6.2
Tasmin 11–4	DDillon	2.3
Carino 11–2	BMarshall	¾.4
Baby Don 11–0	TMolony	1½.5
Sassanian Monarch 11–4	ADGreen	5.6

S.P.: 11/4 PRINCE CHARLEMAGNE, 4/1 Carino, 5/1 Sassanian Monarch, 11/2 Tasmin, 6/1 Madras, 100/6 Baby Don. (Mr L. Lipton) T. Carey, Epsom. 12 Rn 3m 57.15

DONCASTER, Sat., Sep. 15th 1984 (Good to firm)
HOLSTEN PILS ST LEGER STAKES (Gr 1) £110,700
14f 127yds

COMMANCHE RUN 9–0	LPiggott	–1
Baynoun 9–0	SCauthen	nk.2
Alphabatim 9–0	GStarkey	1½.3
Crazy 9–0	WCarson	nk.4
Shernazar9–0	WRSwinburn	s.hd.5

Mont Basile 9–0	ALequeux	12.6
At Talaq 9–0	AMurray	7

S.P.: 7/4 COMMANCHE RUN, 5/2 Baynoun, 7/1 Alphabatim, 8/1 At Talaq, 9/1 Crazy, 20/1 Shernazar, Mont Basile. (Ivan Allan) L. Cumani, Newmarket. 11 Rn

1985
General Accident One Thousand Guineas

Oh So Sharp

I could not possibly leave out the One Thousand Guineas in 1985. This race had everything, supplied by a field of superb quality whose calibre can be judged simply by looking at the subsequent achievements of the contestants. It was a race from pillar to post, with a pulsating photo finish between three outstanding fillies ridden by three classic jockeys.

As if that were not enough, the race saw the launch of Sheikh Mohammed's lovely filly Oh So Sharp, on her quest for the fillies' Triple Crown – The One Thousand Guineas, the Oaks and the St Leger – last achieved by Meld in 1955. Only nine fillies have recorded this historic feat and they include La Flèche, Sceptre and Pretty Polly.

I have been fortunate in being there to 'call' both Nijinsky and Oh So Sharp when they brightened up Town Moor at Doncaster. The Triple Crown starts at Newmarket in the spring and Oh So Sharp was the 2 to 1 favourite for the first fillies' Classic. Trained at Warren Place by Henry Cecil, she had won the Hoover Fillies' Mile at Ascot the previous year when ridden and educated by Lester Piggott.

For 1985 Lester left Henry Cecil as first jockey and his place was taken by Steve Cauthen, in whose hands Oh So Sharp had run a highly satisfactory Guineas trial in the Nell Gwynn Stakes. This race had in the past proved a most reliable guide for the One Thousand Guineas. The field on the day was, however, rich in quality and there was plenty of support for Al Bahathri who had won the

Lowther Stakes at York and then finished a rather unlucky third in the Cheveley Park Stakes.

Alan Clore's high-class filly Triptych, when trained in France had won the Prix Marcel Boussac at Longchamp on heavy ground on Arc day, but had moved to Ireland where she was now trained by Vincent O'Brien's son David. She had just won a good trial at Phoenix Park. From France, Criquette Head sent over Vilikaia, winner of the Prix Imprudence, while Lester Piggott was engaged to ride the Michael Stoute-trained Bella Colora, who as a two-year-old had won the Waterford Candelabra Stakes at Goodwood, and at the last Newmarket meeting had finished a good second to Oh So Sharp in the Nell Gwynn.

Lester Piggott let Bella Colora, normally pretty free, go off in front and they made the running at a spanking pace. They were joined at the half-way stage by Al Bahathri, who also liked to be up in the van, and the tempo was increased still further. At the Bushes these two fillies were still in command with most of the other runners in trouble. Going into the dip Oh So Sharp was only fourth and seemingly getting nowhere. Lester Piggott on Bella Colora on the far rails and Al Bahathri and Tony Murray were still having a battle royal when suddenly, Steve Cauthen at last succeeded in getting Oh So Sharp organised and she began to close on the two leaders. It was a cliffhanger of a finish, for Oh So Sharp was now in full flight and lengthening her stride like a class filly.

Steve Cauthen is a deceptive rider; he seemed to be pacing the filly, not asking for too much too soon but building up to a crescendo, so that in the shadow of the post she was now travelling at her fastest. Neither were the other two stopping – Piggott and Murray were extracting every ounce from their fillies – then right on the line all three fillies crossed it, apparently in a triple dead heat. I was sure Oh So Sharp had won: she was really travelling by the time she had reached the post. Had she made it on time?

Oh So Sharp had got up to win by a short head, and Al Bahathri was second just another short head in front of Bella Colora. It was absolutely sensational, and Steve

Cauthen had in my opinion ridden one of his finest races to get Oh So Sharp up, literally in the very last stride. She had needed every yard of the Rowley mile to win, but win it she had. I felt great sympathy for Tony Murray, who had probably ridden his finest and most athletic finish on the second. He must have thought when he shaded Lester Piggott and Bella Colora that he had it won.

All three fillies in the photograph went on to win their next engagements – Oh So Sharp the Oaks, Al Bahathri the Irish One Thousand Guineas and Bella Colora the Lupe Stakes – while Triptych, who had finished only seventh, beat the colts in the Irish Two Thousand Guineas, the first time that this had ever been done.

After winning the Oaks Oh So Sharp deputised for the injured four-year-old Slip Anchor in the King George VI and Queen Elizabeth Stakes, where she was beaten only a neck by Petoski. Commanche Run beat her by three-quarters of a length in the Benson and Hedges Gold Cup at York. Then came the St Leger, and her chance of the Triple Crown became possible only when Slip Anchor was retired after being injured during his preparation for the King George.

Oh So Sharp was retired to her owner's stud at the end of the season, but her old rival Triptych soldiered on and at the time of writing had clocked up eight Group 1 races in a distinguished career of international racing.

NEWMARKET, Thurs., May 2nd 1985 (Good to firm)
GENERAL ACCIDENT 1,000 GUINEAS STAKES (Gr 1)
£85,647 1m

OH SO SHARP 9–0	SCauthen	–1
Al Bahathri 9–0	AMurray	s.hd.2
Bella Colora 9–0	LPiggott	s.hd.3
Vilikaia 9–0	FHead	¾.4
Stella Grande 9–0	RCochrane	2.5
Aviance 9–0	CRoche	nk.6
Triptych 9–0	PEddery	¾.7
Dafayna 9–0	GStarkey	5.8
Que Sympatica 9–0	MMiller	½.9

S.P.: 2/1 OH SO SHARP, 6/1 Triptych, 7/1 Bella Colora, Dafayna, 9/1 Aviance, 10/1 Antartica, Vilikaia, 11/1 Al Bahathri, 33/1 Devon Defender. (Sheikh Mohammed) H. Cecil, Newmarket. 17 Rn 1m 36.85

1986
Tote Cheltenham Gold Cup

Dawn Run

As one of the worst winters on record relented just in time to allow the 1986 Cheltenham National Hunt Festival to go ahead, there was a possibility that the popular Irish mare Dawn Run could make the meeting rather special if she were to add the Gold Cup to the Champion Hurdle that she had won two years earlier.

The mare's 'sighter' for the Gold Cup ended in disaster and recrimination when Tony Mullins, the young son of trainer Paddy Mullins, was unseated by Dawn Run at the last open ditch during the Cheltenham January meeting. Though Mullins had been Dawn Run's regular rider, he had been 'jocked off' in favour of Jonjo O'Neill for the 1984 Waterford Crystal Champion Hurdle, and Jonjo's greater experience had paid off on the day. Subsequently Tony Mullins had won the French Champion Hurdle and had then been the mare's regular partner in her limited campaign over fences. At Cheltenham, in his exuberance over the mare's first experience of English fences, Mullins rather lost sight of the primary objective, which was to get Dawn Run round safely at all costs. He allowed her to dominate the race from the start and, warming to her task, she put in a massive leap at the ditch after the water jump. She had the field strung out behind her as they approached the last open ditch, always a bogey fence at Cheltenham. Instead of standing back as she had at the previous fence she suddenly changed her mind, put in another stride and clouted the fence hard. Mullins, who rides too short to look stylish, was decanted round the mare's neck on the off side. With incredible dexterity, he somehow landed on his feet and retained hold of the reins.

Had he landed on the near side he would have been far better placed to vault back in the saddle and continue. As it was, while he was getting organised the field swept by and the race was lost. Unbelievably, he then continued some thirty lengths behind the field, no doubt thinking that he would at least school the mare over the remaining fences. In fact the mare did not jump very tidily and the whole exercise as a confidence-boosting outing for horse and rider was a dismal failure. Owner and trainer took it all philosophically, hoping that the mare would have learnt her lesson. The press speculated that once again Jonjo O'Neill would be called up for the big one. In due course the decision was made, and once more young Mullins lost the ride to Jonjo. The latter was only just recovering from a mid-season injury, but he travelled to Ireland to ride Dawn Run in a school round Punchestown racecourse, which did not go particularly well.

As Gold Cup day dawned few tipsters remained faithful to Dawn Run, remembering her relative inexperience over fences, her last race at Cheltenham and the fact that Jonjo had never ridden the mare in a race over fences. Racegoers, starved of racing for most of February, came to Cheltenham in droves. The build-up for the race was enough to give anyone an attack of nerves. But if Jonjo had any they did not show, for from the moment the race was on he made no concessions to Dawn Run's inexperience. They stormed into the lead and set a punishing pace for the first circuit – only the front runner Run and Skip could keep them company – and it seemed to the watchers in the stands that this exceptionally fast pace would invite challengers from the rear as the leaders must inevitably tire.

There was a tremendous splash as the leaders took the water jump. Dawn Run's hind legs trailed through the water, and she then met the fifth fence from home awkwardly, losing her momentum and the lead to Run and Skip. For a few strides she appeared beaten, but running down to the third-last fence she was one of four horses still in the race with a chance; Run and Skip, Wayward Lad and Forgive'n'Forget were her opponents at this point. As the final stages of the Gold Cup unfolded, few could have forecast the drama yet to come.

Jonjo O'Neill had been staying at the same Prestbury Park hotel as Monica and Tony Dickinson, who trained Wayward Lad. In 1983 when their son Michael had saddled the first five horses in the Gold Cup, Jonjo had ridden Wayward Lad into third place. This year it was the Dickinson's stable jockey Graham Bradley who was on Wayward Lad, becoming the protagonist in the build-up to the most extraordinary finish for the Gold Cup, indeed for any race, that I have ever described.

We left the race with three fences to go and with four still in the race with a chance. As they rounded the final turn Run and Skip was still leading, but with Wayward Lad closing and Jonjo driving Dawn Run for all he was worth, the climax was in sight.

Rounding the turn and running to the second-last fence, Jonjo gambled: he asked the mare for a big jump, got it, and was back in contention. Now Run and Skip began to lose his place, but Wayward Lad and Forgive'n'Forget seemed to have the race between them and Dawn Run could really only hope for third place. For a horse that is supposed not to like Cheltenham Wayward Lad suddenly found a yard of speed, and getting away quickly from the last fence he began a run up Cheltenham's 'heartbreak hill' which in any normal year would have won the Gold Cup, for his closest rival Forgive'n'Forget had thrown away his chance by hanging to the right towards the wide open spaces on the standside rails.

Half-way up the final hill Wayward Lad led Dawn Run by at least three lengths, but Jonjo saw that Wayward Lad had begun to drift to his left. It was this imperceptible signal that gave Jonjo renewed hope, and now demonstrated his uncanny instinct for winning races. He told me that Dawn Run never quite gave everything, and so with the leader visibly tiring with only fifty yards to run he switched her to the right of Wayward Lad and bullied her. Inch by inch she gained on Wayward Lad, and with her head down and her ears laid back she gave Jonjo the Gold Cup he so desperately wanted and wrote herself into the history books. Dawn Run broke the course record by almost two seconds.

Graham Bradley, beaten by one length on Wayward Lad, just could not believe it, yet when the horses pulled up his was the first hand that stretched across to shake Jonjo's, followed by all the other jockeys as the horses came back down the course to unsaddle. By now the Grandstand was alight with enthusiasm. Rider and mare received a standing ovation and Jonjo, his hand raised aloft, might just have won an Olympic Gold Medal. Not only had Dawn Run become the first to win a Champion Hurdle and the Gold Cup, she had also snatched the National Hunt prize-money record from the horse she had just beaten, Wayward Lad.

There is always much rejoicing by the Irish when one of their horses wins at the National Hunt Festival. Vincent O'Brien's many winners have been greatly feted after their triumphs, but I doubt if anything has ever superseded the scenes that followed on that day, as Jonjo and Dawn Run made their way round the back of the stands to the unsaddling enclosure at the end of the parade ring. As I watched these incredible scenes on my TV monitor I wondered if they were ever going to get there, for there seemed to be a solid wall of cheering, happy people, all wanting to touch Jonjo and the mare. But it takes two to make a horse race, and at that moment my sympathies were with Graham Bradley and the veteran Wayward Lad. They had set the target for Dawn Run, and to have come so close to victory only to have the race snatched from them so dramatically must have been extremely painful.

Graham Bradley asked me if he could have a cassette of my commentary of the race, which I suspect may be the most memorable of his career. Perhaps he did not believe the result and wanted confirmation; more likely, he was aware that he had been party to one of those rare pieces of racing magic that come along from time to time. I delivered the cassette to Graham at Liverpool, and sent another to Jonjo. I also had my Gold Cup racecard framed for Jonjo to hang alongside the one I had given him for winning the Champion Hurdle in 1983 on this outstanding race mare.

Following this victory, Dawn Run was elected National Hunt Racehorse of the Year for the second time. She had previously won the award in 1983 after her success in the Waterford Crystal Champion Hurdle.

There was speculation that Jonjo would retire from riding there and then, but he did not. Sadly, things did not go well at Liverpool when Dawn Run fell at the first fence in the Whitbread Gold Label Cup. Shortly afterwards Jonjo suffered yet another serious injury when Nohalmdone fell two flights from home in the Scottish Champion Hurdle when in contention. This was Jonjo's last ride, and at the Newmarket Guineas meeting he came along to announce his retirement from the saddle.

The postscript to this glorious moment in National Hunt racing is clouded in sadness. Who would have believed that less than six months after the Gold Cup, the hero and heroine of the hour would again be front-page news? Dawn Run was tragically killed in the French Champion Hurdle, breaking her neck and dying instantly, while Jonjo was stricken with cancer.

Like Bob Champion, Jonjo fought the disease and has emerged from his arduous treatment fit and well; he is now training in Cumbria. When riding he was arguably the most popular jockey ever to don silks. In a profession that has provided many great and popular heroes, Jonjo epitomises the four greatest qualities: courage, skill, modesty and sportsmanship. I just hope I am still around when he trains his first Gold Cup winner.

Dawn Run currently holds two records: she is the only horse to have won both the Waterford Crystal Champion Hurdle and the Tote Gold Cup, and she holds the record winnings for National Hunt racing – £269,083. Between 1982 and 1986 she ran thirty-five times, winning twenty-one races. She fell only twice, at the first fence at Liverpool and at Auteuil when she so tragically ended her glorious career.

CHELTENHAM, Thur., Mar. 13th 1986 (Good to firm)
TOTE CHELTENHAM GOLD CUP (Gr 1) £54,900 3m 2f

DAWN RUN 8–11–9	JJO'Neill	–1
Wayward Lad 11–12–0	GBradley	1.2
Forgive 'n' Forget 9–12–0	MDwyer	2½.3
Run and Skip 8–12–0	SSmithEccles	1.4
Righthand Man 9–12–0	REarnshaw	10.5
Observe 10–12–0	JDuggan	30.6
Earls Brig 11–12–0	PTuck	7
Von Trappe 9–12–0	RDunwoody	8
Cybrandian 8–12–0	ABrown	9
Castle Andrea 8–12–0	GMernagh	10
Combs Ditch 10–12–0	CBrown	11

S.P.: 15/8 DAWN RUN, 7/2 Forgive 'n' Forget, 9/2 Combs Ditch, 15/2 Run and Skip, 8/1 Wayward Lad, 20/1 Cybrandian, 25/1 Earls Brig, Righthand Man, Von Trappe. (Mrs C. D. Hill) P. Mullins, Ireland. 11 Rn 6m 35.30 (record)

1986
THF Prix de l'Arc de Triomphe

Dancing Brave

Since I began broadcasting the Prix de l'Arc de Triomphe (the Arc) on radio, there have been many dramatic moments to describe – Sea Bird's win, the defeat of Nijinsky, Mill Reef's victory for Britain and America – but none surpassed the joy of calling Dancing Brave's sprint through the field to win in 1986.

Dancing Brave had won the General Accident Two Thousand Guineas and had then been quite the unluckiest loser of the Ever Ready Derby that I have ever seen. Re-establishing himself in the Coral Eclipse, Dancing Brave then beat a strong field for the King George VI and Queen Elizabeth Diamond Stakes at Ascot in July, gaining sweet revenge over Shahrastani who had beaten him in the Derby.

The Arc was then announced as the Brave's next target, even though the going at Longchamp in October frequently turned up soft, which would not have suited Prince Khalid Abdullah's beautifully actioned colt. In the event it proved to be the driest autumn for years, and the going on the first Sunday in October was fast.

It is never easy broadcasting big races away from home, and the French radio engineers usually have a fairly relaxed attitude to connecting the lines from Longchamp to London. This year I approached the business with rather more confidence than usual because telex messages had been flashing to and from our Paris office in order to try to prevent similar near-disasters to those of previous years. We were only partly successful. Although we had a willing and efficient engineer from RTF, there was no sign of the TV monitor, nor was it possible to transfer the interviews that we had recorded, for the assorted connecting leads were not compatible with the French sockets.

I believed that we were in for something special, for it was an international field of high quality. The pride of the French challenge was their magnificent Derby winner Bering. The Aga Khan ran four: his dual Derby winner Shahrastani; Shardari, who had won the Matchmaker at York; his Royal Ascot winner Dihistan, who was to be the pacemaker; and at the last minute his Prix Vermeille winner Darara, trained in France, was added. The German champion Acetenango had earned his place in the line-up by winning the Grand Prix de St Cloud, which gave him an unbeaten run of twelve successive victories.

There were many anxious days for Guy Harwood when it was rumoured that the Longchamp authorities were going to water the course. This would have been damaging to Dancing Brave's chances, as rain was forecast in the area for the Arc weekend. Guy had thought of pulling Dancing Brave out of the King George when the ground was yielding for the races run the day before. Guy and Grant Pritchard-Gordon, Prince Khalid Abdullah's racing manager, had arranged to fly to Paris from Goodwood airfield, but to their consternation the field was closed because of fog and they had to fly from Southampton. On arriving in Paris they were astonished to learn that there had been no rain, the authorities had not watered the course and the going was officially 2.5 – léger, the firmest ground since 1980 when the filly Detroit had set up the Arc course record.

It often happened that a British-trained horse went to the Arc with high hopes, only to prove a disappointment on the day. In many cases the Arc had been tacked on to a long, hard season. The late Sir Noel Murless once said: 'The Arc is run three weeks too late for a horse that has undergone a Classic preparation.' Although Dancing Brave had won the Two Thousand Guineas, Guy Harwood had carefully mapped out the colt's programme with just one easy race at Goodwood between Ascot in July and the Arc. The preparatory race at Goodwood could not have gone better – Dancing Brave had shown that he was in top form and his action in the last two furlongs had been breathtaking. Guy, usually pretty keyed up before a big race, went to lunch calm and confident. He told Grant Pritchard-Gordon that he had never had Dancing Brave in better shape and that he *would* win the Arc.

In spite of his record, Dancing Brave was not the Arc favourite in the ante-post market; that distinction went to Bering, who after an impressive win in the French Derby had been saved for the Arc. However, on the day the enormous British contingent present showered money on the Brave, to be ridden by Pat Eddery, and he started the 11 to 10 favourite.

Thanks to the fierce pace set by Baby Turk, a new record seemed likely as the field swept up the hill past the Petit Bois. Yves St Martin, who rode Darara, was later to criticise the rider of his pacemaker Dihistan for not going to the front, but such was the early speed that he was unable to take up a position there. At half-way Baby Turk was still leading, with the Aga Khan's three runners in close touch. Pat Eddery from an outside draw had Dancing Brave lying twelfth of the fifteen runners.

When riding Dancing Brave to victory in the King George, Pat had been concerned when Shardari was able to close on him in the last hundred yards. He was now determined not to make his run quite as early as at Ascot. There is always a risk in coming from behind in a race like the Arc: the downhill bend seems to go on for ever and anyone saving ground on the rails can often suffer interference when the tired pacemakers drop back. The outside track is further, but safer. Before racing began on this occasion, Guy Harwood had gone into the weighing room and asked Pat Eddery how he was going to ride Dancing Brave. Pat had replied, 'I am going to be the last one to challenge.' After hearing those words Guy had turned on his heels and left; he knew the race was as good as won.

So Pat Eddery's skill and nerve were now to be severely tested as he swung into the Longchamp straight with only four horses behind him. As the riders of all the leading fancies now played their hands the Arc could have gone to any one of them, as half a dozen horses in line abreast now faced the final two furlongs. Pat now asked Dancing Brave to quicken and, challenging with an uninterrupted path on the outside of the field, he timed his run to carry him past Bering, who had taken the lead and was running on strongly for home. What happened next was largely missed by Channel 4 viewers, for the Grandstand TV cameraman was concentrating on the leading group. What the viewers missed was the most devastating sprint finish by any horse in a mile-and-a-half race anywhere.

In a hundred yards Dancing Brave was level with the leaders and then he was away, still sprinting, and he passed the post one and a half lengths ahead of Bering, though it looked more like two lengths. Triptych once again took third place, as she had done in the Eclipse (and as she was to do the following year behind Trempolino). The last two furlongs were run in 11.4 seconds a furlong, which is the speed at which sprinters finish. Dancing Brave established a new course record of 2 minutes 27.7 second, knocking 0.3 seconds off Detroit's record set in 1980.

Dancing Brave became only the fourth British-trained winner since 1969, when the Arc had gained its present status as an international event. Not only did Dancing Brave beat a field of the highest class, the manner of his victory put him in the Sea Bird and Mill Reef class. The British visitors present cheered horse and rider deafeningly in the winners' enclosure.

Prince Khalid Abdullah had won the Arc the previous year when Rainbow Quest had been awarded the race in the Stewards' room after he had suffered interference from Sagace. There had been a sour atmosphere on that occasion, but now there was no controversy, just a warm atmosphere of total enthusiasm for a fine horse winning in brilliant style. Even the Head family, who believed that they had a true champion in Bering (subsequently found to have cracked a bone), were generous in their praise for Dancing Brave.

Long after the dust had settled Pat Eddery, who still

had stars in his eyes, was interviewed for BBC Radio by Ian Robertson in the weighing room, just as he was about to leave the course. We planned to use this for the *Today* programme on the Monday morning, but at that stage had no means of transmitting the tape to Broadcasting House. We called on the good offices of the BBC's Paris correspondent, Philip Short, who interrupted his Sunday to open up the BBC studio. I am sure it was worth it.

LONGCHAMP, Sun., Oct. 5th 1986 (Firm)
PRIX DE L'ARC TRIOMPHE (Gr 1) £367,985 1m 4f

DANCING BRAVE 3–8–11	PEddery	–1
Bering 3–8–11	GMoore	1½.2
Triptych 4–9–1	ACordero	½.3
Shahrastani 3–8–11	WRSwinburn	s.hd.4
Shardari 4–9–4	GStarkey	nk.5
Darara 3–8–8	YSaint-Martin	1½.6
Acatenango 4–9–4	SCauthen	2.7
Mersey 4–9–1	FHead	nk.8
Saint Estephe 4–9–4	CAsmussen	1½.9
Dihistan 4–9–4	AKimberley	nk.10

S.P.: 11/10 DANCING BRAVE, 11/4 Bering, 15/4 Acatenango, 9/2 Darara, Dihistan, Shahrastani, Shadari, 16/1 Saint Estephe, 21/1 Mersey, 64/1 Triptych. (K. Abdulla) G. Harwood, Pulborough. 15 Rn 2m 27.70 (course record)

Cauthen's Classics

While writing *The Price of Success* I spent many a morning at Findon with Captain Ryan Price watching the horses work on the Downs. Often he would bellow at a lad riding past, 'Let your leathers down, who do you think you are, Lester Piggott?'

Ryan once said to me that Lester had done racing the greatest disservice by yanking up his stirrup leathers and riding so short, because every racing lad now copied him, with the result that horses had sore backs, the lads couldn't apply 'leg' to a horse and they were very insecure – if a horse bucked or whipped round they inevitably fell off. Ryan partly cured this habit by imposing a fine of £1 for each lad that was unseated (only ten shillings if they held on to the reins!). This money was extracted by the head lad after work and went into the Christmas fund. 'Why oh why don't all lads copy Jimmy Lindley, who had a far better style for the lads to model themselves on – the classic English seat?'

Scobie Breasley, Bill Williamson and George Moore represented the Australian school of jockeyship over here and were among the best jockeys in the world. However, Jimmy Lindley's style was perfection in every department, the very best in British technique – so much more suitable for riding an effective finish on our widely differing courses and for keeping a horse balanced and running straight.

Jimmy was tutored by Tom Masson, who trained at Lewes, to whom he was apprenticed. Life was hard in those early days, for Jimmy found his weight rocketing up and for a while he had to ride over hurdles. He then returned to flat racing and became a much sought-after jockey, winning the Two Thousand Guineas twice, the St Leger and the King George, and the Queen Elizabeth Stakes when he rode Aggressor on the day they beat Petite Etoile, one of the sensations in the history of the race.

One of Jimmy's most important wins was on Precipice Wood in the Gold Cup. They beat the Derby winner Blakeney, on the last occasion that a Derby winner took part in the race. When he retired from riding in 1974, Jimmy joined the BBC Television racing team and his voice is now a familar part of the flat-racing coverage. Sometimes he has joined me in the commentary box to summarise the big races on radio, and I think he enjoyed that task on Derby Day 1987. He took a particular delight and pride in the marvellous victory of Steve Cauthen on Reference Point.

When Steve, the 'Kentucky Kid', first came to Britain in 1979 to ride for Barry Hills and Robert Sangster, Jimmy Lindley acted as his advisor. 'We walked every yard of every course together before Steve rode there, and he very soon began to ride them like an old hand.'

At Salisbury on 7 April 1979 they sloshed their way round the rain-soaked course before Steve's first ride in Britain. It was the worst weather for racing I can remember. It started to rain in the morning and continued throughout the day; the going was heavy, the public walkways were a sea of mud and the electric power failed; there were cohorts of press photographers, and it was a ghastly introduction for the American to the British weather.

Undaunted, Steve Cauthen ploughed through the mud to win the first race on Marquee Universal, thus winning on his first ride in Britain. He had two further rides that day – a second on Ring Lady in the One Thousand Guineas Trial and fourth on Tap on Wood in the Two Thousand Guineas Trial, which was won by Lake City.

Afterwards it was bedlam in the rain and the mud; everyone was trying to interview Steve Cauthen, who handled the whole bedraggled affair with good humour and complete composure. Later, as we tried to push our cars out of the mud bath that had been the car park, many people felt that they might well have seen a future champion jockey, although none, I suspect, realised that they had also seen the winner of the Two Thousand Guineas.

Under Jimmy Lindley's guidance Steve Cauthen soon adapted himself to the immense variety of English racecourses, the changes of going and the incessant travel. At the Newmarket spring meeting, riding in his first English Classic, Steve was fourth on Topsy in the One Thousand Guineas. Two days later he partnered Tap on Wood for Tony Shead – the horse that he had ridden in the mud at Salisbury. Henry Cecil supplied the first two in the betting, the 15 to 8 favourite Kris and the joint second favourite Lyphards Wish at 13 to 2, with Young Generation on the same mark; Tap On Wood was 20 to 1.

The going was yielding and as the race took shape at the Bushes, that famous landmark three furlongs out, three horses drew clear. They were the favourite Kris on the rails, ridden by Joe Mercer, Tap On Wood with Steve Cauthen in the centre, and Young Generation racing with Greville Starkey on the stands side. Steve Cauthen was therefore sandwiched between two of our best jockeys, but as the race drew to its exciting climax it was the American who had the initiative and kept it, for racing all out Tap On Wood beat Kris by half a length with Young Generation a short head away third. It was a magnificent finish – Steve had held on to his narrow lead in the last hundred yards despite the prolonged challenge on either side by Joe Mercer and Greville Starkey, two of the strongest finishers. It was a sign of things to come. Cauthen had won his first English Classic on only his second ride, and for the stable that had brought him to England. In that first season he rode 52 winners out of 379 rides.

1987 Ever Ready Derby – *Reference Point*

In June 1987, nine years later and with almost a thousand English wins to his credit, Steve Cauthen set out on Reference Point to try to win his second Derby. Jimmy Lindley and I discussed the race before the field came under orders, and his assessment of the tactics and the way the race would be run proved completely accurate as Steve set out to make all the running on the powerful, relentless galloper Reference Point.

It had not proved easy for Henry Cecil to get Reference Point fit in the spring, and a sinus operation delayed his seasonal appearance, ruining the owner's dream of the Triple Crown. The Mecca-Dante Stakes at York was the earliest race that Reference Point was forward enough to take in, and as usual Steve Cauthen made all the running. Though clearly needing the race, Reference Point had galloped with zest all the way and in beating the useful Ascot Knight he set up a particularly fast time, 2 minutes 8.25 seconds, the fastest time that the race had ever been run and within 1.15 seconds of Roberto's sensational record time in the 1972 Benson and Hedges Gold Cup, when he had become the only horse ever to beat Brigadier Gerard. Yet Reference Point was not supposed to be fully fit. Neither had the race *appeared* to be particularly fast.

The proximity of the runner-up, the maiden Ascot Knight, beaten one length and running on well, did pose a few questions but Michael Stoute, who trained him, signalled that his Danzig colt would run in the Derby. There was no escaping the fact that the time proved the value of the race as a trial. I never thought any horse would get near to Roberto's record, when his Panamanian jockey, Braulio Baeza, went off at a sprinting pace – 12.1 seconds a furlong.

Steve Cauthen had already won a Derby by making the running two years earlier on Lord Howard de Walden's Slip Anchor. The *Timeform* essayist responsible for the review of Slip Anchor's season in 'Racehorses of 1985' reasearched into the Derby winners who have made all the running.

Hawaiian Sound held the lead in the 1978 Derby until the very last strides and Moon Mountain also made a splendid attempt in 1969 when he was run out of third place. So far as we know Slip Anchor is the first Derby winner to have led from start to finish since Coronach in 1926, and he's the only post war Derby winner apart from Nimbus (who tried to make all but was briefly headed in the straight) and Snow Knight to have led round Tattenham Corner. Slip Anchor equalled Troy's achievement of winning by seven lengths, an official margin of victory bettered only by Shergar, who won by ten.

Slip Anchor's time of 2 minutes 36.23 seconds was fast, but not fast enough to get into the top ten fastest times. What it did confirm was Steve Cauthen's exceptional ability to judge the pace from the front, and in other big races he used this tactic to devastating effect.

Reference Point had already gained a reputation for galloping his opponents into the ground. At Sandown in his second race as a two-year-old he had broken the two-year-old course record for the mile. At Doncaster in the William Hill Futurity, ridden that day by Pat Eddery, he had run his field ragged to win by five lengths. His sole outing as a three-year-old was totally convincing at York, and on Derby Day he was the 6 to 4 favourite, having opened at 7 to 4.

The Race

Reference Point, bred by his owner at the Cliveden Stud at Taplow, was flying the flag for England; no fewer than eleven of the nineteen runners in the field were bred in America. The Cliveden Stud had never before bred a Derby winner, but when it was owned by Lord Astor it had produced five runners-up.

Slip Anchor, bred by his owner Lord Howard de Walden, had interrupted a run of three American-bred colts in Golden Fleece, Teenoso and Secreto when he won by seven lengths in 1985. Slip Anchor had been by Mill

Reef's son Shirley Heights, and Cauthen had exploited that horse's proven stamina with a truly devastating exhibition of powerful front running.

In addition to the favourite, Henry Cecil saddled the active chestnut Legal Bid who had overcome steering difficulties to win the Lingfield Derby Trial. The Two Thousand Guineas form was represented by Bellotto (second) Most Welcome (third, but disqualified for bumping) and Ajdal (fifth after being interfered with by Most Welcome). There were three runners from France: Groom Dancer; Sadjiyd, ridden by Yves St Martin in his last Epsom Derby; and Persifleur.

Steve Cauthen set off at a cracking pace for the first half-mile, obviously trying to run the finishing thrust out of some of his opponents not certain to stay the trip. Water Boatman raced in second place, but supporters of the Aga Khan's colt Sadjiyd soon knew their fate, for after two furlongs he was tailed off. Subsequently we learnt that he had become excited on the way to the start, stirred up by some gypsy ponies tethered on the infield.

Meanwhile Steve Cauthen was still leading at the top of the hill, and now came the crucial point in the race. Many good judges doubted whether Reference Point would be able to act on the downhill run to Tattenham Corner. In 1985 Cauthen had been able to increase his lead here on Slip Anchor, but he found that Reference Point kept changing his legs and he had to hold him together running downhill.

At this point the two French colts were too far behind to take any hand in the finish; Ascot Knight was beginning to fade, Belotto was well behind and was to suffer traffic problems, while Legal Bid had been bumped into and injured. The horse which really threatened Reference Point throughout the last three furlongs was Most Welcome, and as Steve Cauthen found Reference Point's relentless gallop just beginning to become uneven, he sat tight and suffered until the horse was balanced again. This enabled Most Welcome to deliver a really dangerous challenge, while Belotto was making giant strides on the outside, after being hampered and having to switch in his run.

That then was the scenario for the climax of a truly memorable spectacle, as now Steve Cauthen urged Reference Point on. The race had clearly been run at a fast and furious gallop. Could Reference Point sustain it? The answer came magnificently as Reference Point regained his rhythm and went away from Most Welcome and Belotto to win the Derby by a length and a half.

Most Welcome, who had run the race of his life, short headed Belotto for second place and Sir Harry Lewis made late progress to finish fourth. This was the second Derby in three years for Henry Cecil and Steve Cauthen, and it was Cauthen's sixth Classic win. It was a thoroughly worthy win, and the race was run in the second-fastest time in history – 2 minutes 33.9 seconds, only a fraction outside the time set up in 1936 by Mahmoud of 2 minutes 33.8, which had been timed with a hand-held stop-watch.

Jimmy Lindley was enthusiastic about Steve Cauthen's riding.

> He must have a clock in his head; he went fast early on to burst the non-stayers, sat on him down the hill and yet still had enough up his sleeve to finish the race with a final spurt. A marvellously judged race, and it showed that on the right sort of horse you can go all the way in the Derby. He has changed the rules.

Reference Point went on to win the King George VI and Queen Elizabeth Diamond Stakes at Ascot and the St Leger at Doncaster. He then disappointed in the Prix de l'Arc de Triomphe, where he again made strong running before fading in the straight. (He was later found to have an abscess in his foot.) The pace he set contributed to the record time achieved by the winner, Trempolino.

Reference Point has now retired to stud. I would love to have seen him in action as a four-year-old, galloping all the young 'pretenders' ragged. He was an exciting horse, and on that day at Epsom he was superb. So, too, was the rider, who controlled the race from the start and never lost the initiative.

EPSOM, Wed., June 3rd 1987 (Good to firm)
EVER READY DERBY STAKES (Gr 1) £282,024 1½m

REFERENCE POINT 9–0	SCauthen	–1
Most Welcome 9–0	Paul Eddery	1½.2
Bellotto 9–0	PatEddery	s.hd.3
Sir Harry Lewis 9–0	JReid	2.4
Entitled 9–0	CAsmussen	½.5
Mountain Kingdom 9–0	MRoberts	nk.6
Groom Dancer 9–0	DBoeuf	1.7
Sadjiyd 9–0	YSaint-Martin	nk.8
Ajdal 9–0	RCochrane	1.9
Persifleur 9–0	ACruz	1½.10

S.P.:6/4 REFERENCE POINT, 11/2 Sadjiyd, 8/1 Legal Bid, 11/1 Bellotto, Entitled, 16/1 Groom Dancer, 25/1 Adjal, Ascot Knight, 33/1 Love The Groom, Most Welcome, Mountain Kingdom, Persifleur. (L. Freedman) H. Cecil, Newmarket. 19 Rn 2m 33.90

1987
Dresden Diamond Stakes

Ten No Trumps

The appearance of HRH The Princess Anne, as she then was, in the role of amateur flat-race jockey at Epsom in the spring of 1985 made the Farriers Invitation Stakes the most noteworthy race on the card. At the time, the Princess was Master of the Worshipful Company of Farriers and it was to bring publicity to the Farriers' cause that the race was instigated. The Princess underwent a rigorous campaign to become fit enough to ride in a race in public. Her tutor was trainer David Nicholson, and I doubt if anyone ever had a more dedicated pupil.

David already had a good foundation upon which to build, for the Princess was already a superb cross-country rider, having taken part in international eventing, and had won the European Championship on the Queen's gelding Doublet in 1971, in which year the Princess was also voted BBC Television Sports Personality of the Year. Race riding, though, is a very different game and asks searching questions of muscles that one did not even know existed. The Princess regularly went to David Nicholson's stables at Condicote in the Cotswolds to ride work, gaining all the time in strength and confidence. The horse chosen for the Princess's first ride in public was the hurdler Against the Grain.

The Farriers Invitation Stakes was the first race on the card at Epsom on 23 April 1985 to be run over the one-and-a-half-mile Derby course. There were sixteen runners and Against the Grain went off at 12 to 1. Most judges believed that the horse really needed further than one and a half miles, but everyone was waiting to see how Princess Anne would cope with Tattenham Hill and Tattenham

Corner. It was a real media event, with as many photographers present as for the Derby. It must have been unnerving for the Princess 'first time out', but she was very composed and clearly concentrating on getting to the post all in one piece. Throughout the race she kept Against the Grain on an even keel and they were perfectly balanced coming down Tattenham Hill, but once in the straight the leaders had 'flown' and although Against the Grain ran on, he finished fourth, about three and a half lengths behind the winner No U Turn ridden by Elain Mellor.

It was a very promising start, and in the post-race interviews which Princess Anne graciously gave to me and Colin Turner of IRN she said how much she had enjoyed the experience and hoped that she would have the opportunity to ride in other races during the season. The Princess did ride regularly during the year whenever her commitments allowed, and she rode her first winner at Redcar on 5 August 1986 on Gulfland, trained by Gavin Pritchard-Gordon at Newmarket. It was her fourteenth ride, and she was gaining in confidence with every race.

On 'Diamond Day' at Ascot in July, as a curtain-raiser to the King George VI and Queen Elizabeth Diamond Stakes, De Beers Consolidated Mines sponsor a Ladies' Race, the richest of the season and appropriately named after a famous diamond, and the rider of the winner receives a diamond brooch.

In the 1986 race, that year called the Orloff Diamond Stakes, Princess Anne rode Cresta Auction and finished ninth of the sixteen runners. A last-minute invitation to ride the eventual winner, Eve's Error, had to be declined as the Princess had already been engaged to ride Cresta Auction. Michael Stoute trained Eve's Error, and was saddling the winner for the third time in five years. In the winners' enclosure David Nicholson said to him, 'Will you provide a winner next year for *my* jockey to ride?'

So, the following year, the Princess weighed out in the yellow silks with the red diamonds, the colours of Mrs P.L. Yong from Singapore who owned Ten No Trumps – the horse that the master of Beech Hurst had mapped out for his fourth win in the race.

Unraced as either a two- or three-year-old Ten No Trumps, a son of the American sire Nodouble, had run for the first time as a four-year-old in a conditions race at Leicester in April 1987. He was touched off by a head after taking the lead. He did not run again until June, and later finished a good second to the three-year-old filly Tahilla at Newbury, beaten by only half a length.

In the Dresden Diamond Stakes Tahilla met Ten No Trumps on weight for age terms, receiving 11 lb from the four-year-old. Tahilla, the 7 to 4 favourite, was ridden by the very experienced wife of Pat Eddery, Carolyn. Ten No Trumps started at 9 to 1. With the eyes of some 32,000 racegoers and millions of television viewers upon her, the Princess Royal cantered steadily to the post on the soft ground.

Well drawn, the Princess made a good start and raced in second place as It'm For Gala made the running. Princess Anne had gone to Newmarket to ride a gallop on Ten No Trumps, so she knew the horse's characteristics and now, travelling strongly, they took the lead before the turn and hugging the rails swung into the straight with a useful-looking lead which they gradually increased. A furlong out Ten No Trumps had the race sewn up, but now Tahilla made progress from the pack and pursued the leader. The Princess resisted the temptation to look round and risk becoming unbalanced, and Ten No Trumps galloped on strongly to win easily to a standing ovation from the crowd.

It was a most professional performance and provided the television viewers with some delightful pictures of the Princess returning to the unsaddling enclosure to a reception usually reserved for a Derby winner. There were now happy scenes as Her Majesty the Queen, Prince Philip and the Queen Mother all congratulated the Royal jockey, who was now presented with a yellow-gold necklace by Mrs Jenny Wiggin, the wife of Diamond Day organiser George Wiggin.

When the Princess was asked how this win compared with her European Championship, she said that the race had all been over so quickly. Be that as it may, the post-race atmosphere almost upstaged the big race, won later by Reference Point.

As Ten No Trumps stood in the winners' enclosure, those two professionals Michael Stoute and David Nicholson looked pretty pleased with themselves, as well they might. The 'A Team'. One had trained the horse, the other the rider. As Hanibal Smith would have said, 'I love it when a plan comes together.'

ASCOT, Sat., Jul. 25th 1987 (Soft)
DRESDEN DIAMOND STAKES (Ladies Race) £4,546 1m

TEN NO TRUMPS 4–10–0	PrincessRoyal	–1
Tahilla 3–9–3	CarolynEddery	4.2
Commonsidr Gipsy 3–9–6	JennieGoulding	¾.3
Rhondaling 3–9–3	JoannaWinter	2½.4
Water Boatman 3–9–6	PennyHills	4.5
Below Zero 4–10–3	SharonMurgatroyd	3.6
Shannon Cottage 3–9–6	SaraLawrence	7

S.P.: 7/4 Tahilla, 85/40 Water Boatman, 8/1 Commonsidr Gipsy, 9/1 TEN NO TRUMPS, 10/1 Shannon Cottage, 14/1 Rhondaling, 40/1 Below Zero. (Mrs P. Young) M. Stoute, Newmarket. 16 Rn

---

The Finish

On reflection I have been very fortunate in being able to watch the very best in racing over some thirty years from the best seat in the house. It has been an enjoyable privilege to describe great events at Royal Ascot and the Cheltenham National Hunt Festival, Epsom, Newmarket, Goodwood, Aintree and York. The advantage that the radio commentator has over his television counterparts is that while they do half each, he does every big race.

When I took over in 1960 from Raymond Glendenning, the pioneer of sports broadcasting, racing coverage amounted to just 50 races. By 1980 it had risen to 270, while it has now steadied to around 170 per year.

The sport has seen more changes in the last 30 years than in its whole history. It has now become big business, both through the development of the breeding industry, which is truly international, and through the extraordinary growth of betting. Racing remains the most intriguing way of gambling 'the thinking man's gamble'.

Betting hardly enters into these memorable races. These are stories about heroes rather than coups, and in this nostalgic look-back, I have only scratched the surface and there will be those who feel that I have missed out many races which ought to have been included.

I have, I suppose, created a whole library of word pictures of great races, and I know that the personalities who starred in some of those moments enjoy being able to play them again. I sent a cassette of the 1979 Derby to Willie Carson, who I know, when things start to go wrong and winners become elusive, plays the tape again and again. '. . . . Here Comes Troy. . . .' performs wonders for Willie's morale!

The last word comes from 'Banjo' Patterson:

> But all the finest horsemen out – the men to beat the band –
> You'll find amongst the crowd that ride their races in the Stand.

Bibliography

Raceform/Chaseform
Raceform Note-book
Timeform's Racehorses Annuals
Timeform Chasers and Hurdlers
Timeform Perspective
Superform
Red Rum, Ivor Herbert (William Luscombe Publisher Limited, 1974)
The Cheltenham Gold Cup, John Welcome (Pelham Books, 1984)
The Encyclopaedia of Flat Racing, Roger Mortimer (Robert Hale, 1971)
History of the Derby Stakes, Roger Mortimer (Michael Joseph, 1973)
The Flat, Roger Mortimer (George Allen & Unwin, 1979)
The Brigadier, John Hislop (Secker & Warburg, 1973)
Royal Champion, Bill Curling (Michael Joseph, 1980)
The Sea Pigeon Story, Bill Curling (Michael Joseph, 1982)
Monksfield, Jonathan Powell (World's Work Ltd, 1980)
Champion's Story, Jonathan Powell (Victor Gollancz Ltd, 1981)
Men and Horses I Have Known, The Hon. George Lambton (Thornton Butterworth, 1924)
The Race of the Century, Christopher Hawkins (George Allen & Unwin, 1976)
Vincent O'Brien's Great Horses, Ivor Herbert and Jacqueline O'Brien (Pelham Books, 1984)
Prix de l'Arc de Triomphe 1965–1982, Arthur Fitzgerald (Sidgwick & Jackson, 1983)

The Grand National, Clive Graham and Bill Curling (Barrie & Jenkins, 1972)
My Greatest Training Triumph, John Hughes & Peter Watson (Michael Joseph, 1982)
The Story of Mill Reef, John Oaksey (Michael Joseph, 1974)
Lester, Dick Francis (Michael Joseph, 1986)
Ruffs Guide to the Turf
The Collected Verse of A. B. 'Banjo' Patterson (Angus and Robertson, 1921)